Praise for *Starting from Scratch*

"*Starting from Scratch* mobilizes Osnat's contagious energy to develop and articulate a proven strategy to restarting your career. This eye-opening, common-sense, and engaging read weaves the perfect balance of managing change and maintaining your mental health."

Christopher Schembra

USA Today's "Gratitude Guru" and author, Gratitude through Hard Times

"With the dizzying pace of innovation and the convergence of industries, you may have no choice but to reinvent yourself repeatedly throughout your lifetime. *Starting from Scratch* combines storytelling with the fundamentals required to open doors and pursue the unexpected."

Lisa Gable

Former US Ambassador and award-winning author, Turnaround: How to Change Course When Things Are Going South

"*Starting from Scratch* provides practical advice that can help you cultivate the resilience essential for navigating the treacherous seas of change. Osnat Benari has written an accessible and insightful book for these challenging times."

Tal Ben-Shahar

Best-selling author and cofounder, Happiness Studies Academy

"As a fifty-eight-year-old woman who has started from scratch too many times to count, I discovered that *Starting from Scratch* explains what I had yet to put my finger on. 'Scratch' for me came from an awful divorce, job loss, moves, and the start of my business. Osnat's uncanny ability to create a system to empower the start-from-scratch process is raw, real, and relevant no matter where you are for the life changes we choose—and those we don't. Read this!"

Loren Greiff

President, PortfolioRocket

"Starting over can be a very scary process; nevertheless, it's part of life. Osnat Benari takes all of us who are sometimes trapped in lives we don't belong anymore by the hand and leads us into a better future that helps us find and reinvent ourselves again and again. *Starting from Scratch* is as much a practical guide as it is an inspiration."

Darja Gutnick

Cofounder and CEO at Bunch (Business Punk Watchlist 2021), rebel psychologist (Forbes), and podcast host (Teams at Work)

"No matter who you are or how expert you are in your field, everyone starts over at some point. It could be a job, a project, a relationship—things change because humans change. Osnat Benari wonderfully articulates how to best manage these evolutions by integrating skills she learned in business as a product developer with psychology-based learnings that deepen the human skills we need to adapt. Topics like building your own board of directors, challenging someone's mindset, and building resilience are all covered to grow forward with grace, clarity, and optimism. A must-read for anyone who is in the midst of change."

Bobbi Wegner, PsyD

Lecturer in Psychology at Harvard, founder and CEO of Groops, author

STARTING FROM SCRATCH

STARTING FROM SCRATCH

Manage Change like Your Career Depends on It

OSNAT BENARI

Advantage®

Published by Advantage, Charleston, South Carolina.
Member of Advantage Media.

ADVANTAGE is a registered trademark, and the Advantage colophon is a trademark of Advantage Media Group, Inc.

Printed in the United States of America.

10 9 8 7 6 5 4 3 2 1

ISBN: 978-1-64225-297-2 (Paperback)
ISBN: 978-1-64225-425-9 (eBook)
LCCN: 2022914459

Cover design by Megan Elger.
Layout design by Analisa Smith.

This publication is designed to provide accurate and authoritative information in regard to the subject matter covered. It is sold with the understanding that the publisher is not engaged in rendering legal, accounting, or other professional services. If legal advice or other expert assistance is required, the services of a competent professional person should be sought.

Advantage Media helps busy entrepreneurs, CEOs, and leaders write and publish a book to grow their business and become the authority in their field. Advantage authors comprise an exclusive community of industry professionals, idea-makers, and thought leaders. Do you have a book idea or manuscript for consideration? We would love to hear from you at **AdvantageMedia.com**.

To Healey, Libby, and Eliad—my safe place when I'm starting from scratch.

CONTENTS

FOREWORD xiii

MY STARTING FROM SCRATCH xvii

INTRODUCTION 1

CHAPTER 1: 11
Adopt a Learning Mindset

CHAPTER 2: 33
Grow Your Resilience

CHAPTER 3: 61
Build Your Personal Board of Directors

CHAPTER 4: 85
The Spark

CHAPTER 5: 111
What (or Who?) Is the New You?

CHAPTER 6: 133
Bringing Your Vision to Life

CHAPTER 7: 163
Check Your Baggage

CONCLUSION 185

ACKNOWLEDGMENTS 191

ABOUT THE AUTHOR 195

FOREWORD

When I met Osnat, she was fourteen years old; in middle school, she participated in a program I developed and marketed as my first venture. The program taught young teenagers practical studying skills, teaching them methods to study better and absorb information more effectively.

For Osnat, learning at school didn't come easy because the methods used in school didn't fit her personality and learning style. At that time, the school system was less aware of the various learning styles and differences required to teach children with learning disabilities such as ADHD.

In math and other subjects, Osnat's grades were just OK, not great, but she had a deep passion for making that change.

I remember asking the students in my program what they were going to do to change their grades. Osnat stood up and said, "I don't care what my current grades are; I'm going to start from scratch."

Months later, her report card started filling up with A grades across all subjects. And by being introduced to the new cohorts, she became an inspiration for hundreds of students who saw that they too could start from scratch and change their future; it was just a matter of choice, decision, and execution.

Thirty years passed, and Osnat and I are still in touch. Without knowing it, I became a member of her personal board of directors, supporting her when she needed help managing her career.

The most significant and fascinating thing I see in her is her approach to career management.

Starting from Scratch is Osnat's gift to a chaotic world—a world where volatility, uncertainty, complexity, and ambiguity (VUCA) is not a phenomenon only organizations need to deal with.

Each of us is experiencing and dealing with VUCA daily.

Osnat gathers the immense experience she earned in product management and gives each reader a simple recipe for implementation based on the perception that each of us is a product; therefore, managing our career must also adhere to product management methodologies.

The difference is that product management is very realistic. Product management is engineered based on data, predictions, market trends, and more, but our career management includes many emotional elements. Needing to deal with changes, fears, and the will to get fast results is hard because persistence doesn't come easy if you are not used to persevering.

In this book, Osnat comes to a full personal circle. In her humane, warm style, she shares the way to continue starting from scratch and making the right changes and pivots despite the unknown.

When the program Osnat participated in at the age of fourteen ended and her parents saw her report card, her mom contacted me and told me, "You took her and made her change." I remember telling her that I was there for Osnat, but the person who took her future into her own hands was Osnat. She defined the new person she wanted to be and embarked on a new journey without looking back and without letting past failures manage her, and she did it. Osnat changed the story she was telling herself about who she is, and everything changed.

When you read this book, you may feel like Osnat is sitting by your side from time to time. Take that energy, and with the six-step method she developed, don't be afraid to stop so you can change the story you tell yourself. I guarantee you'll change your life and enjoy starting from scratch all over again.

Take this advice: once a year, come back to this book and start your journey, with Osnat by your side, all over again. This is how you'll master managing your career every single time, and you'll be able to make your wildest dreams—those you didn't dare dreaming of—come true.

Gil Peretz

Entrepreneur and TEDx speaker who loves to start from scratch

MY STARTING
FROM SCRATCH

I knew from a very young age that writing would always be an important part of my life. As a kid, I was writing stories and poems, and at the age of fourteen I won a writing competition for a teen magazine that landed me a job working there. I was writing magazine articles and led their celebrity gossip column. Later, I also had my own column in a local newspaper.

At the age of eighteen, I auditioned for the Israel Defense Forces radio station and two Israel Defense Force newspapers, but the army had different plans for me, and I was drafted to a different unit.

My first job after the army was at a professional college, where I wrote several guides: *Tips and Tricks for Microsoft Office*, *Advanced Excel Formulas*, and *Basic Programming Guide for MS-Access*. Yes, that was long ago.

I never got back to my dream of being a journalist. I have never written since. Until now.

The writing process was like good medicine for me—reliving stories of my career and others' and seeing how we prevail. Always.

I hope you enjoy this book and that you, too, heal, get back on your feet, and start from scratch.

INTRODUCTION

I was days away from leaving my home in Israel for the United States to start a new job and a new life when my phone rang.

It was my boss.

After the usual "Hello, how are you?" and some casual small talk, he changed his tone. "Just so you know," he told me, "I just resigned. So I'm not sure you should come to the US."

He shared this bit of information with me as my brand-new tenants were walking through my soon-to-be-former home. A home I was practically giving away, given the rush I was in to get my family settled in the US and start the job I had just shifted my entire life for. I was well past the point where I could stop the process.

"You won't be safe," my now-former boss warned. He talked about my work visa and what might happen to me and my family if I lost my position with the company after moving.

But it was too late. I had made this decision to move our family forward, and in everybody's mind, we were already in the United States anyway. So I told my now-former boss, "As you know, I appreciate your warning me, but I didn't really think you were going to be my boss for life, right? Things change. So, I'm going to head to the United States, and I trust that you chose me for the job and that I can still do it, regardless of who my manager is." As a family, we went ahead as planned, and I hoped for the best. I expected the best, to be honest. I was sure I would find a way to make it work.

But at the same time, there was no question that I was at risk. By the time I started in the US office, a plan was already in place for a successor and we were all in wait mode, knowing that the new manager would come in with a totally different strategy.

When this new manager arrived, he started watching me. Not the way a regular new boss does, to learn what their employees are doing. There were no meetings, but there were plenty of surprise visits to ask, "What are you working on?" or moments when he suddenly joined a conversation I was having with my coworkers. I started to get the feeling that credit for my past work had not been passed along. My new boss didn't trust me.

Finally, after several days of this, I was invited into his office. That's when he said the words I had been dreading:

"So, tell me what you're doing."

Now, I knew at that moment that what I was doing was basically useless. I knew I wasn't producing much that was actually beneficial to my employer. Of course, I was still executing plans we had in place, following the parameters of my job, completing assigned tasks, but for whatever reason—maybe the fact that the person who hired me to do it was no longer there confirming the correct strategy—I wasn't very effective. And I knew it. And I knew I shouldn't hide that fact from my new manager, who had been watching me being ineffective every day.

I had to think on my feet. So I said to my new boss, "I can tell you what I'm doing, but I can also tell you what I *can* do. And they are two different things. And I don't think that since my old boss left, the company uses my talents correctly."

My new manager was intrigued. "Great," he said. "So, tell me what you can do." We had a very candid conversation, during which I laid out what I saw as my role in the company and what I could do for them.

After I was finished, my new boss said that he saw my eyes light up when I spoke about what I could do. "And then," he went on, "when you tell me what you are doing, it dies. So how about I give you a project? Let's see you light that fire around this project. And if you do it well, you stay, and if you don't, I'm going to send you home."

This wasn't a simple project. It was a proof of concept to a whole strategy he wanted to carry out—and he gave it to me to execute. I understood it was an all-or-nothing task, one I must carry out flawlessly, on time and on budget.

That was the moment I knew I was going to have to start from scratch.

This new project that I had wrangled for myself was a real one, but it was also, obviously, a test. I had one chance to prove that I still belonged in that role, and if I failed, all the things my former boss had warned me about were going to happen. If my dreams for our new life in the United States were going to come true, I was going to have to rebuild myself to be the person I needed to be to deliver on this new project for this new boss.

My walk home took about twenty-five minutes, and I allowed myself exactly that amount of time to pull myself together. I couldn't come home to two children who didn't want to stay in this strange new country where they didn't know anyone, to a husband who was just figuring out his new career, to a new home and everything else that was new and unfamiliar and add this additional level of stress and uncertainty to the equation. My family was (and is) my safe place. They are everything good in my life, and I needed to keep it that way. So I walked home feeling this intense pressure to find a solution so that this new life we were just starting to build could continue and blossom, the way I envisioned it would when I decided to take that job. I was very, very deep in my head, working through this problem … when out of the blue, I heard a male voice say, "Smile, lady."

I turned toward the voice, and it was a homeless person. A man who was obviously down on his luck was looking at *me* and couldn't help noticing how upset and stressed out *I* was. That forced me to put things in perspective. I hadn't lost anything … yet. I was much luckier than this man. I still had my home and my family and even my job. I wasn't being given a death sentence. What I was being given was an opportunity.

For those working in tech as a product manager or in any other position, starting from scratch should be a given. Our business is the epicenter of a state of affairs that's being called VUCA—which stands for volatility, uncertainty, complexity, and ambiguity. Technology is all about the pursuit of the next revolution, which isn't exactly an environment where calm is the norm. Tech companies are all about scale, which comes with growth, change, and adjustment, and tech workers like me need to be agile and adapt quickly to changes. For example, a colleague who works at another company was recently at a meeting where employees were asked to talk about and define their company values. Everyone pitched in to come up with a list of values, and eventually somebody said, "Buckle up and get ready for a wild ride." Which means basically, "We encourage flexibility," right? Flexibility, resilience, openness to change … all good stuff. So, unsurprisingly, that particular value generated a lot of positive response. A lot of people were in total agreement, saying things like "Yeah, it's so crazy. It changes here all the time—it only makes sense that one of our values should be 'Deal with it.'"

But my friend's response was a little different. He said, "Well, I don't know any successful tech company that doesn't change. And then I would actually argue that if you need to be told to 'deal with it,' you don't belong here."

Whenever I worked for a company, it was pretty clear that when we were doing really well, it was always pretty crazy. We were always in the middle of either acquiring a company or getting a big influx of capital from investors who wanted a part of our success. When we weren't doing that … well, *then* it was calm. But that was about it.

And that's the thing.

The moment you have to start from scratch, when you have to embrace change, is where you find opportunity.

> The moment you have to start from scratch, when you have to embrace change, is where you find opportunity.

Embracing change, instead of hiding from it or fighting it or pretending it isn't happening, opens you up to all the possibilities that change might generate. Embracing those possibilities is how companies grow. It's how people grow. Even when the opportunity comes in the form of something you don't want, it's still a chance to build something new and better.

I know, because starting from scratch is how I built my career. I have been through several reorgs so far, and I truly believe the reason I'm still standing is not my amazing talent or my quick wit but simply the fact that I've learned how to do it. I have developed a set of tools that work and a system for putting them to use.

And I'm sharing that system in this book.

Because the reality is, the need to start from scratch isn't limited to product managers like me. Major change can happen in your life regardless of your choice of career. In fact, it's more likely that it will than it won't. According to the career website Zippia, the average person will change jobs twelve times in their lifetime.[1] Add other workplace changes like management or ownership changes, shifts in roles, and the natural evolution of any business, and it's clear that your odds of having to deal with some sort of major upheaval over the course of your career is pretty close to 100 percent.

Maybe starting from scratch is exactly the jump start you need.

And starting from scratch isn't only a professional thing. On the personal front, according to the Centers for Disease Control and Prevention, an average of just under 750,000 couples will divorce this year in the US (or, more specifically, in Washington, DC, and the forty-five states that report their data).[2] Relationships end, people move, interests change … and we haven't even touched on the "Great Resignation;"[3] all these things, too, can result in a need to start from scratch.

But maybe starting from scratch is exactly the jump start you need.

Walking home that day after the meeting with my manager, when that homeless guy told me to smile, I realized that what happened next was ultimately up to me. I was in control. I just needed to adjust my mindset and become the person I needed to be.

1   Chris Kolmar, "Average Number of Jobs in a Lifetime [2022]: All Statistics," *Zippia*, April 5, 2022, https://www.zippia.com/advice/average-number-jobs-in-lifetime/.

2   "Marriage and Divorce," Centers for Disease Control and Prevention, accessed June 30, 2022, https://www.cdc.gov/nchs/fastats/marriage-divorce.htm.

3   Ranjay Gulati, "The Great Resignation or the Great Rethink?" *Harvard Business Review*, March 22, 2022, https://hbr.org/2022/03/the-great-resignation-or-the-great-rethink.

That's when I realized, *I can do this.*

And you can too.

Over the next seven chapters, I'll share everything I've learned, both as a product manager and as a human being, about starting from scratch, either by choice or of necessity. I'll also share the inspiring stories of other people who have undertaken this same journey—often multiple times. They include the following:

- Hilla Bakshi, founder, HaMeetupistiot

- Carrie Collins, chief advancement and strategic planning officer at Philadelphia College of Osteopathic Medicine and founder and CEO of H.O.W.

- Melissa Cohen, founder and owner of MBC Consulting Solutions

- Sabela Garcia Cuesta, NFT artist

- Jonaed Iqbal, podcaster and founder of NoDegree.com

- Eugina Jordan, VP of marketing at Parallel Wireless

- Mariana Kobayashi, author of *Productivity Might Be Killing You* and founder of #kobayashirunningchallenge

- Lisa Mayer, cofounder of Boss Beauties and founder of My Social Canvas

- Phyllis Njoroge, author of *From Fraud to Freedom*

- Ashwini Panse, CRO of North American Clearing at ICE

- Kathryn Parsons, chief digital operations officer at MACH9 Digital

- Liliana Petrova, CEO and founder of the Petrova Experience

- May Piamenta, founder of Vee

- ⊘ Maria Rosati, founder and CEO of Eminence Communications Inc.

- ⊘ Landon Sanford, founder of a stealth company

- ⊘ Mae Singerman, administrative project manager at Showing Up for Racial Justice (SURJ)

- ⊘ Prabhdeep Singh, chief growth officer at Clover Health

- ⊘ A few others who preferred to remain anonymous

Whether you're adjusting to a new company mission, looking for a new job, or reentering single life after the end of a relationship, you'll learn to embrace the open, learning mindset that will keep you on top of your game and ready for what's next. You'll discover tricks to develop the resilience you need to handle the stress that comes with change. You'll learn to recognize the external and internal triggers (also known as Sparks) that alert you in advance that change is coming and how to prepare for what may be next. You'll imagine a different version of yourself based on who you need to be to thrive in your new reality—and then build that person from the ground up (a process you will likely need to go through more than once in your life). And finally, once the work toward becoming that person is underway, you'll discover tools to help you get to know, understand, and care for the inner you.

With homework at the end of each chapter to help you put each lesson to practical use, this book is a step-by-step guide you can turn to over and over again, whenever you have to start from scratch.

So let's get started right now.

CHAPTER 1:

Adopt a Learning Mindset

When I was creating the outline for this book, it was hard for me to decide what step to focus on first. In reality, most of the steps in this process are things you can work on (and will be working on) simultaneously, especially in the beginning of the process. But there's one thing you can begin doing right this minute, without any sort of preparation, that will help you start from scratch. In fact, you're doing it now, just by reading this book. You are seeking out new information, which means you are, at this very moment, operating from a learning mindset.

Learning is essential to me as a product manager. I must learn everything I can about my people, the market, my competitors, and my users. I need to be constantly updated and in the know, because the landscape is always changing. My job is to come up with solutions to user problems that either don't exist or are created when there's a new disruption, trend, or technology. Being in constant learning mode allows me to foresee change so I can prepare accordingly.

Learning is also essential to my process. I use YouTube and LinkedIn Learning, and I follow LinkedIn, Twitter, and Instagram hashtags. They have some great content and features as well as thought leaders I respect. I've also downloaded several "quick learning" apps like Club House, Blinkist, and Uptime as well as industry-specific apps, and I watch videos and talks and read blogs so I'm really, really informed—again, because it's so important to stay on top of every new development.

Hilla Bakshi rearranges her LinkedIn and Facebook pages to serve her learning mode. She follows certain pages and people and engages in posts that help her learn and grow in her areas of interest.

To be honest, I haven't read a single non-work-related book in the past ten years, because there are so many great books focused on my line of work. If I feel I need to learn more about a topic, I read whatever I can find on it (or, better yet, I listen to it—more on why later). I've also read the same book, *Hooked*, by Nir Eyal, seven times … so far. This book is very relevant to my line of work because it's designed to help the reader make their products more habit based. It's basically a guide to building products that are connected to the user's everyday habits in a way that creates value and stickiness.

When I read this book for the first time, that hit me like a bolt of lightning. It was the first time it occurred to me that I needed to actually look for and study the habits of my users. That when I build something, I need to build it as close to the habit I'm trying to tap into or shape as possible so my customer will learn to associate the habit with using my product. That way, when the inevitable competitors came knocking at their door, my customers wouldn't care—because my product is sticky.

Every single time I read that book and work through the steps of the Hooked Methodology, it opens my mind to new possibilities. It inspires me ... *Wait, there are more habits, there are more ideas, there are more innovations ...* and every time I read it, I come up with a new capability. It works like magic for me. Honestly, I know the book by heart, so I could probably go through the exact same process without it. But reading the book is an essential part of the process, because that's what helps me shift into a learning mindset.

. . . .

When Sabela Garcia Cuesta and I worked together at WeWork, I had no idea she was an artist at all ... until I started seeing her work on Instagram. So how did this onetime techie wind up being labeled "the psychedelic Picasso" and gain fame for drawings that are a bundle of joy and a celebration of color? It all comes down to NFTs—and a learning mindset.

As a child, Sabela was a self-described nerd, always had good grades, and was very competitive. One day she realized she memorized her school notes in colors and drawings. But that was as far as it went. While she defines herself as a born artist and admits to having unlimited creative ideas daily, she remembers growing up hearing things like, "You'll never be able to make it," or "If you are a full-time artist, you will be very poor and have a life full of struggle." So she chose to work in tech instead ... until she discovered NFTs.

Talking with Sabela, you would think she's been part of the

world of NFTs since its inception. In fact, she learned it all very recently—and all through doing.

After leaving WeWork, she decided to start from scratch as an entrepreneur. She launched her own CBD brand, which she named Art District, which included developing every aspect of the brand herself. That included drawing more, which unleashed those talents she had kept hidden, which led to her getting invited to shows and galleries, which led to her selling her art and occasionally being asked to lead remote creative workshops during the COVID-19 pandemic.

She was first introduced to the NFT world while visiting Art Basel in Miami. The idea hit home with Sabela because, while she loved making art, she never saw herself working alone in a studio. Getting into NFTs allowed her to do so much more: create, grow a community, and earn money doing what she loves.

Even though Sabela's first NFT experience led her to actually lose money, she considers it part of her learning process and refers to it as her "tuition cost." In fact, the blog post she wrote about the lessons she learned led to her being invited to the What's Next Wall Street show, which in turn has led to her selling even more art. All because she let herself fail—which meant letting herself learn.

. . . .

So ... What Exactly Is a Learning Mindset?

Webster's defines learning as "gaining knowledge or understanding through study [like reading a book], instruction [like listening to a podcast or watching a video] or experience [like taking a class or actively putting a program into practice]." A learning *mindset* is one in which you're actively seeking out knowledge or understanding by whatever method you can. It also means paying more attention to the world around you and taking in more information from it rather than blocking it out (more on that later). It means being curious, asking questions, and listening before you talk. It means being willing to doubt decisions, even your own, and making an effort to look at things from all sides.

In other words, yes, it's giving yourself a lot of extra work. But I promise you, that extra work will be worth it in the long run.

When you open yourself to new knowledge and new understanding, it makes you better at whatever you do and more prepared for whatever changes might be coming. If there is a chance you may need to start from scratch in the near future, if you seek out and stay open to the relevant information, you'll probably know in advance. Then you can plan accordingly.

That's a big part of the reason I think I was able to save my job when I moved to the United States after my boss quit. When I started in the role, I wasn't just focused on the tasks I needed to accomplish each day, each week, each month. I was focused on survival. My now-former boss had already warned me I was in layoff risk. So I asked myself questions like *Why am I doing this?* and *Is there a better way?* At the same time, I paid attention to my surroundings. I made sure I was up to date on what was going on in my industry and kept my eyes and ears open to take in information about what my team and the company were trying to accomplish, what was being done to achieve that, and, most importantly in my case, what wasn't working and could be done better. I then considered my own skill set and strengths to determine where and how I could make things better.

As a result, when that inevitable question from my boss about how I was spending my days finally came, I was ready—or as ready as I could be. I already knew what I was doing was not working and that starting from scratch, in one way or another, was almost an inevitability. So instead of simply rattling off the daily tasks that I already knew were getting me nowhere, I showed my new manager that I was actively learning my job and figuring out how I could best contribute. That alone probably bought me the opportunity to start from scratch with that same company instead of in a new job someplace else.

Escaping the Execution Mindset

In that particular instance, I was lucky. Because I was new to the team (not to mention the city, state, and country), being in a learning mindset was a natural state for me. We tend to put ourselves in a learning mindset whenever we start something new so we can understand what we need to do and how to do it. In my case, I also needed to figure out what my role was and how to hold on to it despite the change in management—as quickly as possible. And I was able to do that successfully.

However, once you survive the initial transition and adjust to your surroundings, it's easy to let your learning mindset go. After all, once you've figured out how to do your job, the goal isn't to spend your time learning—it's to actually do the work you were hired to do. So most people's instinct is to shift to producing as much and as well as they possibly can. I count myself among those "most people." I know how easy it is to get laser focused on making progress, moving forward, doing everything humanly possible (and sometimes more) to meet your goals. As a product manager, I am under constant pressure to produce, and sometimes, in order to meet that demand, I have to block out the world around me so I don't get distracted. This is what I call "execution mode."

Execution mode is the mode in which I spend most of my time. It's kind of like home for me. It's so obvious in everything I do that not long after I started with a new company, my supervisor met with me and said, "You're like a machine! Every single hour of the day, I find something from you, or I get an email from you." And I had to admit she was right. I am like a machine. Once I get going, it's hard to get me to stop.

But this particular machine does have an off switch. And you need one too. Because no matter who you are, you have to continue to learn your job. It doesn't matter how much experience you have or how good you are at what you're doing right now. You must constantly put yourself in a position to learn new things because the world is always changing, and at some point, in some way, the way you approach your job will need to change along with it. If you never switch back into a learning mindset, you're going to miss the cues that it's time to make that change. But beyond that, whenever you take the time to learn something new, you benefit from it. It adds to who you are, what you know, who you know, and what you can do.

> **Whenever you take the time to learn something new, you benefit from it. It adds to who you are, what you know, who you know, and what you can do.**

So how do I—and you—find the time to fit all this learning in? How can we switch out of an execution mindset and into a learning mindset? I do what a lot of highly successful people do: I put it on my calendar. I skim content on a daily basis, but I also bookmark things I should research more deeply, and I actually schedule time to shut down. I book half a day just to take in new information. That's when I listen to podcasts, read about my industry, meet new people, and do whatever else I need to do to stay on top of my game. I know that if I don't—if I don't force myself to shift into learning mode every few weeks—I will be so busy executing that I will miss some of what I need to know to stay relevant and remain competitive.

Not to knock execution mode. We have it for a reason—it's great for when you really, really need to get stuff done quickly. Then again, when exactly do you *not* need to get stuff done quickly? Not very often in my world. That's why execution mode can be so all consuming. You can execute, execute, execute to the point that you forget to shift out of it, to the point where it's almost like putting blinders on. And while those blinders are great when it comes to blocking out distractions, they also block information you need to know to function at your highest capacity. That's why you need to remind yourself periodically to take a break and spend some time educating yourself. If you can keep your eyes and ears open to what's happening around you no matter how busy you get, you won't miss crucial indicators that change is coming.

· ·

Vee founder May Piamenta has spent her entire career in a learning mindset—because her very first job was as CEO. She started her first company at the age of twenty, recently raised $12.5 million, and is now on the Forbes 30 Under 30 list. But before that, she had to learn everything from scratch. "I started a company without knowing things like how to do a QBR, what are KPIs or OKR, how to pay salaries. To learn, I met with many founders, and every founder I met, I asked for their time, and I asked this question: 'What now?' Founders were happy to share their learning and experience on what I should be solving for now versus later."

May learned to be spontaneous and opportunistic, which led her to great places. Today, her two-year-old company employs almost forty people, and as CEO, May sees continuing to learn as a crucial aspect of her role. "Continuous learning is very different from what you are taught to do when you grow up," she explains. "When you are little, you are taught to think that you need to learn to become an expert, and this implies that once you are an expert, you give answers and don't ask questions, but I genuinely believe that if you don't learn, you waste your time."

May walks the talk. She dedicates five hours each week to meeting other CEOs for one-on-one consultation and knowledge sharing. She also set up her own KPI to assign three mentors from her network to each Vee executive team member. "I just know that without my mentors showing me the road, I would have never been successful."

We Are Not the Frog

Most of us have heard that old story about the frog in the pot of water. You know, the one where, supposedly, if you put a frog in a pot of boiling water, it will immediately jump out, but if you put a frog in a pot of room-temperature water and slowly heat it, the frog will stay in the water until it's cooked? I recently watched a TED Talk by the organizational psychologist Adam Grant that was centered on the point of that story, which is that the frog doesn't notice its environment changing until it's too late. It's a popular metaphor for how we humans fail to notice things changing around us until we can't do anything about them. We get so mired in execution mode that we block out everything else, to the point where we don't realize that what we're doing isn't actually working anymore.

Years ago, I consulted for a company that was working on a very mature product. They were leaders in the market, but the CEO saw one of his teams as stagnant and hired me to inject some new life into it.

The team was working on a product that from my perspective just didn't make sense. So I asked them, "Why are we working on this?" Their answer? "Because we committed." "Great," I said, "but when was that?" It turns out they had committed to this enormous project two years before, and while they were busy trying to bring the product to life, the landscape had completely changed, to the point where the thing they were working on was no longer relevant. The fact that the company had made a decision to pursue the project two years earlier was not reason enough to continue—but since everyone had their heads down in execution mode, nobody could see anything beyond the tasks in front of them. There was no one taking in the 360-degree view, keeping up with the changes in their environment so they could determine when going in a certain direction or pursuing a certain path no longer made sense. It took an outsider (me) stepping in to see what they could not and bring it to their attention. Otherwise, they would have stayed in that particular pot until they boiled.

By the way, Adam Grant concluded his TED Talk by revealing something kind of surprising. The frog-in-the-pot story isn't even true. Yes, the frog will stay in the pot for a while, but once it starts to feel the heat, its survival instinct will kick in and it will jump out and save itself. In other words, the frog jumps, but we don't.

When we're stuck in execution mindset, we stick it out until it's too late.

. . . .

One morning I stumbled upon this post from an entrepreneur and founder named Landon Sanford. I was amazed by his perseverance. He wrote the following:

> I quit my job. I'm starting a new company. Ideally, I'm hoping that this was my last "real" job. Correction: this will be my last real job. I am going to keep starting things until something works out. I don't care if it takes months or years—I'm going to be a founder. I've only had failures so far with start-ups. But at this point, another failure doesn't scare me; regret is the bigger fear in my mind. Regretting not reaching my full potential or regretting a day where I look back at my life and wonder if I played it too safe. So, I'm taking the leap. More failures to come. "The biggest risk is not taking any risk."

When I contacted Landon and told him I was writing this book, he giggled and said, "I wish I'd had a book like that when I started. Starting from scratch is very lonely and something we entrepreneurs need to do all the time."

Like many people I interviewed for my book, Landon started working early and discovered the power of learning by doing. Growing up in South Carolina as a teen, he had a summer job offering shuttle pickups to and from the beach. He made great money from tips. Postgraduation, he dabbled in many different areas, from investment banking to door-to-door book sales, which built the "rejection stamina" he says he needed to have as an entrepreneur. That stamina only grew when he applied for seventy jobs and got rejected by all, but a knee injury and an eight-month recovery period led him to set a goal. "No TV until I start a company," he declared. And then he did it—and raised $1.5 million for it, too.

Despite his early success, that start-up, like so many, didn't continue to grow. He decided to close shop and take a corporate role, but after landing a job with Google, he realized he couldn't stay there. "Once you taste the taste of freedom," he explains, "nothing else tastes the same." Since then, he has launched many start-ups and raised money for them all. And a learning mindset has been essential to all of them.

When Landon first decided to trade his salaried job for the uncertainties of entrepreneurship, he realized from the very beginning he needed to learn to be self-sufficient. There may not have been a team in place, or any funding to hire that team, but for Landon, waiting is never an option. I asked what he discovered he needed to learn and how he went about learning it. This is his list, word for word:

- ➔ "Needed to learn design > took design courses."

- ➔ "Needed to learn how to be a product manager to better work with developers > took product management classes and read product management books."

- ➔ "Realized I needed to be better at public speaking > trained and set a goal to have a TED Talk."

Landon's learning mindset is part of his growth, and according to him, the best way to learn is by "getting into the mud." He knows and understands the founder's way and attributes his persever-ance to not having a plan B: "Just like the Dark Knight jumped without a rope," he says with a laugh.

Staying Aware

Adopting a learning mindset isn't only about taking time out to read a book or listen to a podcast. It's also about maintaining a level of awareness of what's going on around you. In other words, it's about keeping those execution mindset blinders off, at least most of the time, and continuing to take in as much information as possible. It's just another kind of multitasking, and it's a necessary one. Whether you're comfortable in a role you think will last forever or uncertain about what's coming next, you need to constantly listen to the market, to your leadership, and to the leading experts as well as the up-and-comers who are bringing new ideas to your field. You also need to look for opportuni-ties to increase your knowledge and stay ahead of the curve. When you do, you may discover an opportunity to start from scratch on your terms. Even if you don't, you'll be better prepared to do it on someone else's terms.

Look for opportunities to increase your knowledge and stay ahead of the curve.

At one point in my career when things were really in flux, I basically created a position for myself. The media business at AOL, where I worked, was stable but had plateaued for some time. I was concerned for our future survival under a big brand such as Verizon (who acquired AOL) and was concerned for the future of my role as well, especially since Verizon had just bought Yahoo. If things didn't change, we were not going to grow, which meant that eventually, in some way, what I was doing would no longer be relevant. One way or another, I was going to have to start from scratch. So my goal was to do whatever I could to control what form that restart would take and try to keep it at the company where I was currently employed.

At that time, I headed product for the video group, a cross-company technology stack that allowed me to know the organization very well. Verizon then owned over ten media brands, all of which were my internal customers and stakeholders.

I asked myself, *How do I put a stop to this and make us future proof?* Being in media, I considered how media would be consumed in the future and what we were not doing to prepare for that. What technologies did we not have access to that could help us make that leap into the future? I learned about different technologies that Verizon owned and didn't, and then I went to the CTO of the company and said, "How about we actually think about the company in five to ten years? And we start building things that might be very small right now but in the future will be a big bet for the company?"

But I didn't stop there. I also positioned myself as the ideal person to oversee this new project. I said, "There are plenty of great ideas on how to add more value to the company and make it more profitable, but who executes them and who makes sure these ideas are validated and relevant?" And guess what? Since I was the person who proposed a way to build something better, he said, "Okay, you're right. We've already started discussing this in management meetings, so go and build a plan, and we can then talk about it and see if that's a valid role."

I built a plan, a strategy, and an org chart. I set goals for what I would accomplish at thirty-, sixty- and ninety-day timeframes, defined the challenges I expected the role would encounter, and estimated the budget needed.

Two weeks later, I presented him with my proposal. I had to answer some hard questions and argue for some decisions I'd made, but eventually I got the okay to start my new role as head of research and development.

I was able to start from scratch at the same company by creating that role for myself—which not only helped me but also helped my company stay innovative and future proof. Had I not taken the time to learn what was going on in my industry and think through some long-term solutions, I might have been laid-off, because the business I was in at the time was shrinking, not growing.

. . . .

What's more challenging than starting from scratch? Starting from scratch as a new leader. It's the first time you don't have someone always there to tell you what to do and how to do it. Your manager is usually so senior they've forgotten how to coach you, and you quickly learn why they say, "It's lonely at the top." Which is why, when Liliana Petrova started from scratch, she decided to invest in a professional leadership coach to help her find her path.

This was not an easy journey. As Liliana explains, "A coach that matches you and your style is not easy to find, and when I finally found the right one, he was only available weekends. On top of that, he had a cat, and I'm allergic to cats. But for several months, I would wake up early on weekends, take my allergy medications, and head to his office—that's how dedicated I was to growing myself."

For Liliana, one of the most valuable exercises was identifying and writing down her values.

"Many people learn about leadership from courses, HBR articles, and rarely do people decide this is an investment you need to be committed to. I learned that leadership is a belief system; who you are is important. *Leader* is a noun, but when you want to grow into a leadership role, you need to know the adjectives you want to add to it. It was an amazing gift to me. I still have my notes, and I return to them when I feel challenged."

What's Your Learning Style?

Shifting into a learning mindset is about more than keeping your eyes and ears open for changes in your environment. It also means making a consistent, conscious effort to educate yourself, meet with relevant people, and bring your skills up to date by taking in the latest information about your industry. This is where entering a learning mindset can be overwhelming for some people. There are so many ways to take in information right now—podcasts, video blogs, webinars, books, mastermind groups, articles, classes, and on and on and on—it can be hard to determine which ones are worth your time. After all, you only have so many hours to spend outside the execution mindset. You want to make that time count and make sure the information you take in is relevant and that it actually sinks in and sticks. In order to do that, it's helpful to understand your learning style.

Different people take in information in different ways. Even the definition of learning specifies three different methods: study, instruction, and experience. Those represent three different learning styles—taking in information on your own, being taught by someone else, and learning by doing. And if you're like most people, you're more comfortable and more successful learning through some methods than others.

Today, learning styles are represented by several models, encompassing anywhere from three to seven different styles. One of the most popular models is used in the VARK Questionnaire,[4] which was developed to help people determine which learning style or styles are most natural for them.

The letters in VARK stand for four different basic types of learning—visual, aural, reading/writing, and kinesthetic.[5] I will explain below how each of these types of learning works, using a scenario we've all faced—needing to learn how to get to a place we've never been—to demonstrate.

Visual learners take in information they can see in a form other than words. They respond well to pictures—things like video, diagrams, charts, and graphs that illustrate concepts. So, if you want to get somewhere you've never been and you're a visual learner, the best way for you to find your way would probably be to use a map that *shows* you where you are and where you need to go.

Aural learners take in information through hearing and listening. This is one of my preferred methods of learning. Aural learners like me like to have concepts explained out loud, even if they're the ones talking themselves through a process. Hearing the words helps them sink in; therefore, audiobooks, podcasts, and lectures are all great tools for aural learners. If you're an aural learner and you want to get somewhere, your best bet is probably to ask someone for directions or listen to instructions from your GPS that *tell* you how to get where you're going.

Reading/writing learners take in information through language. They process what they read and/or write and remember it, and they

---

4   "The VARK Questionnaire," VARK, accessed June 30, 2022, https://vark-learn.com/the-vark-questionnaire/.

5   "Learning Styles," Florida State University, accessed June 30, 2022, https://ace.fsu.edu/sites/g/files/upcbnu296/files/Study_Strategies_by_Learning_Styles.pdf.

prefer to take in information on their own, like in book form or in print on a website, rather than have it presented to them. As a reading/writing learner, you would probably print out or write down directions to a strange place, which helps you *process* the information, and then follow those directions while you walk or drive.

Kinesthetic learners take in information through their experiences. They learn by *doing*, so any occasion they are able to take action, like a class where they learn by completing various tasks or the opportunity to "shadow" a coworker in order to learn a new job, will work well. If you're a kinesthetic learner, the best way to find a new place is to ask someone to physically take you there.

Did you see yourself in any of these learning styles? Or maybe you saw yourself in more than one area? This is true for a lot of people. Although one type of learning may be more dominant for you, most people use a combination of styles to take in information. So when it comes to pursuing opportunities for learning, understanding your learning style can be a sort of guide to what might work best or be easiest for you. It doesn't mean it's a hard-and-fast rule of what to do and what not to do when it comes to learning, but it will alert you to where you might benefit from some modifications.

There are hacks to make your learning more effective by adapting it to your style. For example, if you want to listen to a podcast or TED Talk even though you're not an especially strong aural learner, consider taking notes if you learn better through reading and writing, or by participating and doing something active. If you're a kinesthetic learner and are having trouble following written instructions, ask someone to show you how, or see if you can practice something new by volunteering or doing pro bono work for an organization or a cause you care about. There's an organization in tech called 48in48 where a bunch of volunteers come together for forty-eight hours and are exposed to forty-eight nonprofits that need help. People with design experience, product experience, and engineering experience all come together and build for that pod. It's a way to give back, but it's also a way to gain experience, exposure, and knowledge.

Of course, it's also fine to take in a podcast or TED Talk or read an article and just enjoy the experience of learning for what it is, knowing some of the information will sink in regardless. As an aural learner, I also find interviewing people who did the thing I want to learn about and discussing their experience helps me learn by "almost" doing.

Now that you have some idea of what the different learning styles are, take some time to think about yours. Do you love listening to podcasts, or do you find yourself forgetting what you've heard after they're done? Do you like to be shown how to do things, or do you prefer to read the instructions yourself? Think about what works best for you—not only in terms of what you enjoy but also how you know you will retain the information. This is what I want you to focus on when you do this chapter's homework.

Identify Your Learning Style

You've already put yourself in a learning mindset by opening this book. Now I want you to put what you've learned in this chapter into action by zeroing in on the best kind of learning for you. Since you're starting from scratch, now is a perfect time to make sure your learning is on track.

1. Identify your learning style, and be aware of what works for you: look into the different learning styles, search for the VARK quiz online, and get a sense of the best way to get information to sink in and stick with you. My learning style is:

   _____.

2. Select the topic you want to know more about or the subject you wish to accelerate your knowledge in.

   Write it here: _____.

3. Select a slot of time to dedicate to learning (not executing). This can be half an hour every morning or night or a chunk of time during the week. This will be your new habit. In 90 days it will be a fun habit, and to make sure that happens,

be sure to block this time on your calendar or set an alarm on your phone. Write your time slot here:

_____.

4. Make a list of learning resources: find some books and blogs, make a YouTube playlist of interesting videos or TED Talks, research helpful podcasts or apps. I am amazed by how effective newsletters are for me, so I'm sharing this tip as well: search for relevant newsletters and subscribe to them. Research which hashtags are relevant to the topic of your interest, and follow this hashtag on social media.

5. Search for thought leaders in your space, follow them on social media, and read their content.

6. Search meetups, events, and communities in the area of your interest. Being part of a learning community will make it feel less like work and make you a more rounded expert in the field.

7. Lastly, see if someone you know can help you learn more about the topic you selected. Connect with them over coffee or video call, and compare notes on how they stay on top of their game.

In the next chapter, we'll look beyond the learning mindset at another essential tool you'll need to develop in order to successfully start from scratch: resilience.

CHAPTER 2:

Grow Your Resilience

A while ago, one of my teams was going through some changes, and some of my people were really struggling with the process, blaming the company leadership for lack of direction and strategy. I kept telling them, "Listen, it's not this company—it's this industry. It keeps changing. You need to be resilient."

I truly believe resilience is basically a requirement in the tech industry, and probably for the workforce in general. It's definitely the number one reason I've survived and thrived in what basically amounts to a professional life defined by perpetual chaos. To be honest, I've always been pretty resilient, but that doesn't mean there wasn't room for improvement. Early in my career, while I was still in Israel, I worked for a company that shut down. Then, for several years, I worked for another company that kept going through reorgs. And I found the experience completely traumatizing.

I was always the person who had to keep coming back to redo the work, onboard my new boss, and then they would reorganize the company again, and then again. I had seven bosses in three years, and every single time it was on me to onboard the new manager. It really was an impossible situation.

I kept getting my heart broken over and over. Every time, I invested in my manager, I invested in relationships and building my credibility, only to have to start again, and again, and again. I was constantly starting from scratch, and I was not enjoying the process. It was hard, and it was exhausting. So I finally decided the best solution was for me to remove myself from that environment, quit that particular job, and start my own company.

Despite all the drama I had witnessed and been a part of, I was on really good terms with everyone at the company I was leaving. So they asked me to stay for a few months, just until the end of the year, while they adjusted to the transition. In return, they offered me six months of severance pay.

This opened a door for me. While I intended to start my own company, there was definitely some risk involved in that. But with six months of salary, suddenly it seemed a lot less risky and so much less stressful. I could afford to take the time to ramp up my clientele and not feel pressured. Even better, my former employer stayed on as one of my clients after my transition time was up. Everything was falling into place. I signed many more clients and started to feel confident that my new business was going to make it.

That's when one of those clients made me an offer to come on board and work for their company full time.

This was absolutely the last thing I wanted. The whole reason I started my own company was to avoid the heartbreak associated with all the reorgs and firings and management shifts that came from working in tech. I wanted to have some control over what happened to me in my professional life. I wanted to choose my own customers and surround myself with situations that were positive and didn't break my heart. I wanted to be able to relax a little bit, not in terms of working less or not as hard but just maybe in experiencing a little less turmoil while I did it.

Was that too much to ask?

When I told all this to my client, he told me his feelings were hurt. He sarcastically said, "So you don't want to work with me?"

"No," I explained, "I like working with you, the company, and everyone I work with. That's why you're my customer! And I would love it to stay this way." And so it did … for a few months. But then he started pushing me again to come work for him and his company. He began checking in with me weekly, saying, "What do you want to close shop and come and work here? What do you want? What do you want? What do you want?"

What did *I want?*

That started to become an interesting question.

It was becoming pretty clear that this person was willing to give me basically whatever I wanted to close my company and come work for him. *Whatever I wanted.* That's a very tantalizing prospect. I was talking about it with my husband, and about what "anything I wanted" could mean. And suddenly it hit me. I said to my husband, "How about I just say what I *really* want?"

And what I really wanted was to move to the United States.

This was a different kind of dream than starting my own company. Starting my company was almost a way to escape from trauma, or at least to try to grab a little bit of control in an uncontrollable field. Maybe it was more of a survival tactic than a bona fide dream. But going to the US? That was actually worth giving up all the control I'd gained and rolling the dice. Moving to the States was something I'd had in the back of my mind for years, ever since a friend from the army and I swore we were going to move to New York City together once we finished our service. Now, this company that was so desperate for me to join its staff happened to have an office in Manhattan.

Could I? Should I?

I did. I asked for what I wanted, and I got it. And after a year, once again everything was falling into place. I had my new job lined up in the US, I had new tenants ready to rent my apartment, I moved my amazing, wonderful, non-risk-averse husband and not-entirely-understanding kids halfway across the world for *my* dream …

And that was when my boss quit.

That was when I really had to learn how to be resilient.

By moving to the US anyway, I had put myself in a corner. I couldn't just leave and start my own company if things got ugly. I was in the United States on a work visa, and my work visa was tied to that specific job and that specific company. So I knew when I decided to go ahead with the plan despite my ex-boss's warning that I needed to do whatever I possibly could to keep that job. I needed to stay present and awake to everything that was going on around me while at the same time learning my new role and while also finding a way to navigate the changes that came with my new manager—*no matter what.*

I was going to have to start from scratch, but if I was going to stay in the States, I needed to find a way to start from scratch on my terms. I think resilience was the secret sauce that allowed me to do that.

Okay, So What Is Resilience?

Basically, resilience is the ability to bounce back from adversity. It could be adversity like getting a new boss right after starting a new job, or losing a job or a relationship, or having your company fail, or getting sick, or not getting something you worked really hard for, or a million other things that we all have and/or will experience in life. That's what makes resilience so crucial. Bad things happen to everyone. Resilience is what separates the people who survive and thrive from those who get left behind.

Have you ever been fired? So was Steve Jobs, from the company he founded (although he was eventually able to win his way back in). Lost a competition you worked really hard to win? That happened to Beyonce Knowles on *Star Search* when she was nine. Michael Jordan famously failed to make his high school basketball team, Colonel Sanders had his chicken recipe rejected by over a thousand restaurants, and Starbucks CEO Howard Schultz was turned down by 217 of the original 242 investors he approached.

> **Bad things happen to everyone. Resilience is what separates the people who survive and thrive from those who get left behind.**

But they didn't give up. They were resilient. Which is why you've heard all their names and know their stories. They made things happen, even when they didn't happen right away. They didn't let disappointment stop them from moving forward. When you're not resilient, life happens *to* you. You're a victim of outside circumstances. Life is beyond your control, and there's nothing you can do about it.

Look at it this way. When my boss quit, I could have said, "I can't go to the US—it's too risky." Probably a sane person would have said that, but I didn't. I could have gotten depressed when I got to the US and my new manager started and it became clear that he wasn't impressed with me. And if I had done that instead of actively looking for a solution to my (and the company's) problem, I probably would have lost that job. Either way, I would have wound up back in Israel.

It would have been a thing that "happened to" me. Instead, by doing everything I could to make something happen, I managed to hold on to my dream. And I've been able to build a career and a life here.

· ·

When it comes to starting from scratch, Kathryn Parsons is a pro. She started a new job in a new country while not speaking the language, and just as she was starting to see success from her efforts, she started again in a new city midpandemic. Most of her career changes have been doubly hard, as she has also been starting from scratch on a personal level. As a result, she could probably write a book just about resilience.

"I come from a socially conservative family, I am a high-functioning autistic, and I identify as bisexual," she explains. "You can imagine how hard it was to find acceptance." In fact, Kathryn was not diagnosed with autism in early childhood, so her family assumed she was developmentally disabled with a speech impediment. Her intelligence wasn't acknowledged until she was able to find her voice through writing and extensive speech therapy. Despite her parents setting the bar low and, when she succeeded, pressuring her to attend a state school for college, she insisted on attending college out of state and raised the money she needed through scholarships.

But the challenges continued. And that's when Kathryn's resilience was crucial.

"My parents had a very different plan for me. They got frustrated with my independence and in my sophomore year suddenly demanded that I change to a more 'practical' major and move in with my brother. When I didn't do as they wanted, I ended up losing their support. Their 'our way or the highway' ultimatum left me homeless. I slept in my car and at friends' places and washed at public bathrooms until I managed to save enough to have a place of my own. It took me seven years to graduate college, as I paid for my own choices. Doing all this taught me I can do anything."

When asked what her advice is for other people who may be facing similar challenges, she says, "Each person needs to find their inspiration. One can focus on what went wrong or focus on solving the problem. Sometimes it's better to start fresh and make the past just a stepping stone toward success rather than suffer in silence because of the fear of future failure."

Part of Kathryn's resilience is her healthy approach to failure and rejection. "When you reach a point when something is broken," she explains, "there's no point in thinking it's your fault. It is important not to continue on the same path, because it will stay broken if you do. You cannot underestimate the power of having a choice. The choice is always better than having no agency and decisions made for you."

The book *Failing Forward*, by John C. Maxwell, has been a particular inspiration for Kathryn. She even recommended I read it. When I told her the term failing forward was an interesting concept, she said, "Don't focus on that—focus on the subtitle, which says *Turning Mistakes into Stepping Stones for Success*. For me, it means I can always focus on what went wrong, but if I want to start something new, I need to make the past a stepping stone." Or, as Mr. Maxwell himself says in *Failing Forward*,

If you really want to achieve your dreams, I mean really achieve

them, not just daydream or talk about them, you've got to get out there and fail, fail early, fail often but always fail forward. Turn your mistakes into stepping stones for success.

Why Resilience Matters

We all face disappointments in life. Most of us will even face tragedies. Often these things really are beyond our control. But that doesn't mean every single aspect of them is out of our hands. We can control how we deal with them. When things go wrong, what matters most isn't what just happened or why it happened, it's what happens *next*. What you do, how you react after something bad happens will determine where that event takes you.

And here's the really amazing part. Resilience is more than the ability to bounce back from disappointment, or bad news, or changes in plans, or any of the bumps that pop up in the middle of your road to happiness. Because that bounce also gives you a secret superpower. It doesn't just keep you on track toward achieving your goal or getting through a rough patch. It actually makes you stronger. Each time you bounce back from one of those speed bumps, you have an opportunity to make adjustments on the fly without losing your momentum. You learn where your weaknesses are so you can shore them up. You determine what's not working and take steps to change it. And as a result, you bounce back better. The entire time you're dealing with a setback, you're maneuvering yourself into a better position to start from scratch instead of wallowing in whatever just ended.

> **Resilience is like a muscle. The more you flex it, the stronger it gets.**

Resilience is like a muscle. The more you flex it, the stronger it gets.

That's why people who are resilient tend to have better outcomes in life. According to the American Psychiatric Association, in the workplace, resilient people experience more job satisfaction, feel happier while on the job, are more committed to their jobs and workplace, and are more engaged.[6] An article in the American Psychiatric Association's workplace newsletter explains that "raising resilience contributes to improved self-esteem, sense of control over life events, sense of purpose in life, and improved employee interpersonal relationships."

. . . .

For Hilla Bakshi, resilience means staying connected to herself, especially during times of change. She likes walking on the beach, and you'll find her there every day at 6:30 a.m. She takes that walking time to think, set her intentions, and keep her mental health strong.

. . . .

On the other hand, when you are not resilient and you face a setback, you can lose focus, to the point where you become ineffective. So if your job is at risk and you lose resilience, you could wind up in a position where you're even more likely to lose that job. Not that there's any shame in losing a job. If it happened to Steve Jobs, it can certainly happen to anyone. Again, time after time, what matters most is what happens next. The people who come through adversity the best and who survive all the ups and downs are the people who are resilient.

---

6   Ewuria Darley, MS, "Resilience: A Strong Workforce Needs It," American Psychiatric Association, accessed June 30, 2022, https://www.workplacementalhealth.org/mental-health-topics/resilience.

Entrepreneur Landon Sanford once posted the following: "I've still only had failures so far in start-ups. Low moments—like running out of funding, being fired, going below minimum wage, letting teammates go, making the wrong decision, etc. But since I quit my corporate job, my plan has been to keep starting businesses until one works. And that will be this one. Failure is not as scary as people think it is! There will always be swings and misses—it's okay."

Landon admits resilience is part of his identity and that he has tried many ways to build his mental health. Last year he read over thirty books, and these days he likes to start his mornings with quiet reflecting on his day ahead. That's what keeps this entrepreneur resilient.

The Hidden Cost of Low Resilience

After experiencing several reorgs, I've seen what a lack of resilience can do to people. I've watched colleagues become deeply, deeply sad with a heaviness they couldn't shake. It's almost like the life and joy had been squeezed out of them, to the point where they just went through the motions. I've known others who live in constant fear of the next reorg, of possibly being laid off, to the point where they have trouble focusing on the work they need to do that will keep them from being laid off. And I get it. After all, I was the person who started her own company because she couldn't handle another reorg (fun fact: it turns out I could).

The recent global COVID-19 pandemic and economic crisis spawned a lot of research on the subject of workplace trauma. I dug into it and discovered numerous posts and articles about people suffering from a form of PTSD called posttraumatic layoff disorder, and I wound up doing some extensive research of my own on the subject. I learned that while workers are less likely to be studied than other groups who frequently suffer from PTSD, they are highly likely to experience it, both as a condition of the job—as experienced by, for example, policemen and firefighters[7]—and after either losing a job or surviving a round of layoffs. *Psychology Today* detailed the symptoms of what it called "layoff survivor syndrome" in a recent article titled "Layoffs and the Stress Response." It discovered that a round of layoffs produces aftereffects, including diminished functioning at work, a downbeat environment, and, most distressingly, stress-response symptoms from sleeplessness and anxiety to heart attacks.[8]

As you can imagine, after all the reorgs I've been through, I have personally experienced layoff survivor syndrome, a kind of survivor's guilt that affects those people who are left to pick up the pieces after a reorg or round of layoffs.[9] I have been that person more times than I'd like to remember—including a time when one of the reorg changes was that everybody was let go but me. I couldn't help wondering, *Was I forgotten? Or did they keep me for a reason?* People who survive a reorg or a round of layoffs have to deal with things like the pain of missing their coworkers, the discomfort of learning new routines, and the resentment of power structures beyond their control, all while being regarded as the lucky ones. Trust me—having been there, I didn't always feel so lucky!

---

7   Erene Stergiopoulos, et al., "Interventions to improve work outcomes in work-related PTSD: A systematic review," *BMC Public Health,* October 31, 2011, https://www.ncbi. nlm.nih.gov/pmc/articles/PMC3219578/.

8   Ray B. Williams, "Layoffs and the Stress Response," How to Fulfill Your Potential, Blog Wired for Success, September 7, 2009, https://www.psychologytoday.com/us/blog/ wired-success/200909/layoffs-and-the-stress-response.

9   Susan M. Heathfield, "How to Cope When Your Coworkers Lose Their Jobs," *The Balance Careers,* February 27, 2020, https://www.thebalancecareers.com/ how-to-cope-when-coworkers-lose-their-jobs-1918595.

We'll take a closer look at how to deal with posttraumatic layoff disorder (PTLD) and other types of career stress later in the book. What is important to understand right now is that PTLD is trauma just like PTSD but with a career focus. And like PTSD, until you deal with it, it will follow you wherever you go throughout your career. It will shape your relationships, experiences, and performance at every job you have. And it can break you, increase self-doubt, and trigger feelings of imposter syndrome. I've known people who couldn't even continue in their own professions, who worked for years in a field with passion until one last layoff or one last reorg broke something deep inside them.

Clearly, I was also one of those people, especially early in my career. But I learned, especially after I wound up almost losing my job in America. I realized that the challenges I face as part of my life are okay, and can even be beneficial, if I approach them with the right mindset. If a change changes me in a positive way and moves me toward growth, how can it be a bad thing? Resilience helps you look for those opportunities to stretch yourself and grow. When you're faced with challenges, even when there is no obvious opportunity, you grow simply by using your resilience muscle to power past them and on to the next thing in your life.

> **Resilience helps you look for those opportunities to stretch yourself and grow.**

My First Reorg

Maybe I developed resilience early because I needed to have it early. When I was fourteen, I entered a writing competition in Israel where the winners got an opportunity to publish in a teen magazine. And because I really, really wanted to win, instead of one submission, I sent ten. And I think I made my point, because the editor of the magazine contacted me. She said, "Listen, I really like your writing; we're going to publish one of your pieces. But we are also doing auditions to write for our magazine. What do you think?"

What did I think? I thought it sounded pretty awesome!

I applied and got accepted, and I started writing for the biggest teen magazine in Israel as one of a group of nine young writers between the ages of fourteen and eighteen. I wrote human interest stories that would appeal to a teen reader like me—things like what it's like to be the girlfriend of a soldier, about an Israeli girl who was acting in Hollywood movies, about a kid that got HIV from a blood transfusion and was ostracized because of it (this was a long time ago!). I even got to interview celebrities for a celebrity column. I loved it. I worked really hard and was making really good money, especially since I was still a child. I figured my life plan was set. I had found my purpose—I was going to be a journalist! Heck, I already was one!

And then all of a sudden, after about a year, the newspaper changed its editor-in-chief.

That was the beginning of my first reorg.

This new editor-in-chief came with lots of big ideas for new ways to do things. And one of the things he decided he wanted to do in a new way was the teen magazine I wrote for. He wanted it to be a bigger, better magazine. Hey, no argument from me! Of course I wanted the magazine I was working for to be bigger and better. Unfortunately, he felt the key to achieving these goals of increasing size and quality lay in two major changes:

1. Each magazine would now have a monthly "theme."

2. All of the teen journalists would be fired and replaced with professional journalists.

In other words, I lost my job. At fifteen, I had already been downsized.

You can imagine how heartbroken I was. I could not believe it, because I was doing so well. How could something so terrible happen? It just wasn't fair …

BUT … this is a chapter about resilience. And resilience isn't about whining about how unfair something is, even if it happens to be unfair. Resilience is about what happens next.

So I didn't cry and complain. Or maybe I did cry and complain, but it wasn't the only thing I did. I also decided there was no way I was going to give up my beloved job without a fight. So I wrote a letter to the new editor-in-chief. And I did it using a strategy. I didn't write to him as a former employee whining about how mad or upset or sad I was that I'd lost the job that I loved so much. I didn't even ask to get it back. Instead, I wrote to the editor-in-chief as a consumer of the teen magazine, explaining *why* what he was doing was, from the perspective of one of his readers, wrong. I focused both on the theme idea and the new, all-professional staff and why I thought they wouldn't work at all and were a terrible idea—from a reader's perspective.

When I finished, the letter was around three pages long. I sent it to the editor-in-chief, and I also copied my editor at the magazine. Then, because this all happened during the summer, I went away on vacation with my parents and kind of forgot about the letter.

When I came home from our trip, there was a message on the answering machine (this was before everyone had cell phones). It was the editor-in-chief. He said, "I really appreciate the letter that you sent me. I would like to talk to you." I thought, *Oh, shit*. And after that, there was another message on the machine, this time from my boss, the editor of the teen magazine. She said, "I don't know what you did, but everybody's back. There's an editorial meeting next Sunday.

You should come."

Being resilient didn't just get me my job back. It got the entire team's jobs back!

Now, I'm not saying that just by being resilient you can automatically save your team from a round of layoffs. I certainly don't have that power, or I would have avoided many of the experiences that inspired this book in the first place. The truth is, I don't always get what I want—if I did, I would be a journalist right now. That dream ended prematurely when I applied for a position as a journalist in the army and they turned me down! Even with all my experience at the teen magazine, I had to take a different army job, something that was not in any way a part of my life plan. And while I fought the decision as hard as I could, I didn't win that battle. No amount of resilience could get the people in charge to change their minds.

However, resilience did make dealing with my disappointment in not getting what I wanted easier. Instead of moping about my shattered dreams and the career plans that had been derailed (or at least delayed), I switched my focus to getting the most out of the position I wound up with, in intelligence. That set me on the path that would eventually lead me to my career in tech, to my dream life in the US, and to writing this book.

Part of resilience is knowing you're not "there yet." There really is no "there" at all, because life keeps changing. So a change in plans doesn't have to mean the end of the world. It can mean new opportunities. It can mean *better* opportunities. When you don't waste time falling apart, you have more energy to focus on what's going on around you and to make the most of it.

Nothing Stops the Rhythm

If you know anything about WeWork, it's probably that a few years ago the company was tech's biggest scandal. But when I joined, I joined a super-successful, financially healthy, hypergrowth start-up about to go public.

Toward the date we were supposed to go public, I was ready, because I was starting to feel the itch to grow (more on that in chapter 4). I had already started to talk about what was next for me and my team. I didn't have all the details, but I assumed that we would have more money and we would have more attention and pressure to perform, so we should plan to do more. And I specifically remember saying, "We should become a larger digital platform so that we can support all of WeWork members."

But we didn't end up going public. Instead, we ended up on the front page with a giant scandal. And it happened in hours. I saw Adam in a town hall one day, and the next morning he was gone.

When I found out Adam had been removed, I texted my boss. Little did I know that he, too, was having a conversation about leaving the company the following morning. I survived the initial purge. However, it was obvious that the next thing coming would be a very large, very painful round of layoffs.

The first thing I did was collect my team, along with a few others. Because some of them didn't have a manager anymore—they had reported directly to my now-former boss. So I told them, "I'm doing a meeting with my team, if you guys want to join."

Once I had everyone together, I said, "Listen, I don't know what's going to happen. And I can promise two things. One is that for now, all of us have a job. I wasn't told anything else. And I will be the one who will update you as soon as I know. I'm not hiding anything. I just really don't know. And I'm going to figure it out, but we all have a job. That's all I know. And the next thing I can tell you is that we had a plan this morning and yesterday and the day before, so how about, until someone tells us not to, we just execute on that?"

So we kept going. At the same time, I had to work on lists of people to lay off if and when the time came and try to decide how it would affect the work we were doing. I began to wonder if I should actually launch things that were in the pipeline or put them on hold. And I came to a decision: "Nothing stops the rhythm."

I knew I would need to handle the consequences of, for example, launching something and then having to lay-off the person who managed what I just launched. I knew we might all have to work overtime just to catch up and figure out how to manage the project moving forward. But I knew that the price of further affecting everyone's mental health, and of losing the rhythm that got us where we were, would be greater.

As a team, we had developed a way of working together that kept propelling us forward. We had a united focus. Yes, if we took the risk, launched something, lost key people, and wound up not knowing what to do, it would be difficult. But I knew it would take us less time to recover if we didn't lose the rhythm that had kept us on track in the first place. Just to confirm my initial impulse, I did a quick pros-and-cons check. Every time, the biggest con was always losing the rhythm. Overall, it would have cost us the most. Although we'd have to face the consequences of moving forward, I felt like we would be in position to recover faster simply because we didn't lose the rhythm.

Let me try to explain what I mean in a different way. Remember the first *Wonder Woman* movie? I definitely do—especially one specific scene in the movie that really sticks with me. Wonder Woman is running at full speed toward a target, totally exposed on the sidelines to all kinds of danger. But she keeps running straight ahead. She's so focused on the task at hand that she doesn't even blink. She does frown, indicating that yes, she's aware of what's happening around her, but she continues to run.

Nothing stops her rhythm.

I found this scene so inspiring that I showed my team members a still of it at a meeting. I told them, "A lot of stuff will happen, a lot of noise. It's not that we're not bothered. Of course we are. You can see in her frown that she is, too, but she doesn't blink. She doesn't close her eyes, and she just runs."

The crazy thing is, when I saw that scene in a work context, I noticed something I didn't remember seeing when I saw the movie. When I saw the image frozen, I noticed that Wonder Woman was in color and everything else was in black and white. When I realized that, I said to my team, "How relevant this is! It's just what we're doing here, because you only paint what you do, what you are responsible for, what you can affect, and what you can change. And then everything else you've colored differently so that you don't lose the rhythm."

Later, when we faced more hard times, more reorgs, and more changes, whenever the team started to lose momentum, I would put the image back on the screen again. I did it so often it became an inside joke. *Do you want to bet she's going to put that picture up again?* Maybe the team was cynical about it, but hey, it worked. Everyone remembered the image, and we had a good laugh—but more importantly, we all remembered what we were going after, personally and as a team.

. . . .

Lisa Mayer is the cofounder of Boss Beauties, a women-led global initiative that creates opportunities for girls and women through cutting-edge collaborations, including Web3, NFT, and more. She is also the founder of My Social Canvas, which provides mentorship and scholarships to the next generation of women and girls. Both of these projects have required Lisa to tap into her stores of resilience.

For starters, Lisa and her husband, Anthony, founded Boss Beauties in the midst of the pandemic. "For eight weeks, we barely slept! We worked incredibly hard on building the community first and foremost as well as our following—the Discord community. We immersed ourselves entirely in Boss Beauties. We had to learn and research a lot, work long hours, and we did all this while having a newborn."

The pandemic also affected My Social Canvas, because no one was meeting face to face, meaning Lisa wasn't able to run the mentorship events that were at the core of her business. Resilience at this point in her career was imperative.

"As an entrepreneur, change is constant, and the challenges never stop. This has led me to pivot often and learn to be extremely resilient. Anthony, my brilliant husband, came up with the NFT idea behind Boss Beauties. BAYC was already taking off, and he came up with the 'Boss Beauty,' which represents a woman who can be whatever she wants. This is the idea that Boss Beauties is rooted in. It's our mission to educate and empower the next generation of women and girls through strategic collaborations that help them achieve their dreams."

Lisa eventually turned My Social Canvas into a nonprofit, enabling her to focus on Boss Beauties and the work she's been passionate about for many years. "Boss Beauties has opened up the door to impact, educate, and create more opportunities for women and girls, which has always been my core mission. We can now do more global virtual events and create an expansion that reaches more people—resulting in better programs, collaborations, etc."

Part of the reason Lisa was able to pivot was that she has learned to be resilient in the face of change.

"This is woven into my entrepreneur DNA. As entrepreneurs, we are not afraid of change, taking risks, and learning new things. In fact, we thrive on it. With Boss Beauties, the worst that could have happened was to lose eight weeks of hard work. But even that had a silver lining, as I would still learn something new and act on my challenges. There is no chance that you lose if you let yourself learn and try."

Building Your Resilience

But what if you're not particularly resilient? What if you are one of those people who, when the pressure is on, tends to fall apart? What if you're already suffering from PTLD? My advice is to relax, take it one step at a time, and work backward—something we'll deal with in a later chapter. For now, remember that nobody is born resilient. We all come into this world totally helpless, dependent on our parents and communities. Our resilience develops alongside other aspects of our psychology, like our self-esteem, based on our life experiences and the people around us. So it only makes sense that some of us are going to come out of our formative years more equipped to deal with adversity than others. Having parents, teachers, and peers who teach us how to fail, who support us but at the same time make us pick ourselves up when we fall, is invaluable. I count myself among those people who have had that kind of support. But I also know plenty of others who were not so lucky. And that's okay, because resilience is a skill that can be built, a muscle that can be developed.

We all have the capacity within us to build our resilience and take more control over our lives instead of simply letting life happen to us. The American Psychological Association suggests the following strategies[10]:

1. **Connect with others.** Sometimes trauma can cause people to self-isolate and cut themselves off from friends, family, or coworkers. Spending time with like-minded people who are empathetic and compassionate reminds you that you're not alone. Plus, you can get ideas, support, and help working through issues just by talking to other people. But don't wait until something bad happens to reach out—start building your network now, whether you "need" it or not. That way, when adverse events happen, your network will already be there for you. You never know who might know the right person or have the perfect words of advice to help you through a tough situation.

2. **Take care of yourself physically, mentally, and emotionally.** That means getting enough sleep, avoiding unnecessary stress, exercising, eating the right foods, and generally keeping yourself in good shape. Because when you're not depleted in any of these areas, you're stronger and more able to deal with adversity when it comes (which it will), plus you're more ready to hit the ground running when

---

10   "Resilience," American Psychological Association, accessed June 30, 2022, https://www.apa.org/topics/resilience.

it's time to start from scratch. The American Psychological Association also advises avoiding relying on coping mechanisms with negative side effects, like turning to alcohol, stress, or food to numb unpleasant feelings.

3. **Find purpose.** The more things you care about, the more things that matter to you, the less any one thing matters. And there are numerous ways to bring more purpose into your life. You can volunteer and help others get through their own struggles, which also builds connections and self-esteem. You can set and work toward some realistic, achievable goals that will give you a sense of control and accomplishment. The point is to have a reason to get out of bed in the morning and start a routine. When bad things happen, try to be proactive as opposed to reactive—when you face a problem, try to take your emotions out of it and instead ask yourself what you can do to find a solution. And look for opportunities for self-discovery. Getting through a traumatic event or experience can reveal strengths you didn't know you had and open you to new perspectives. It may even inspire you to take your life in a completely different direction.

4. **Embrace healthy thoughts.** Focusing on the negative can blind you to all the opportunities and possibilities around you. Remember to keep things in perspective and try to react to setbacks rationally—as I've said throughout this chapter, bad things happen to everyone, not just you. The difference is how you deal with those setbacks. Accept that change is a part of life and that you may need to let certain things go, but that opens you up to new things and experiences. Keep a positive outlook by focusing on what you want instead of

what you fear. And learn from your past by looking at how you handled hard times previously and determining what you would have done differently.

5. **Seek help if you need it.** If the above strategies don't get you where you want to go, if you're feeling stuck, or even if you're doing okay but would like some expert support working through an issue, refer to a coach or consider a licensed mental health professional for guidance.

. . . .

Prabhdeep Singh was a colleague of mine at WeWork. He was with me in 2019 when our manager left the company. We had a few minutes to sync with him and say goodbye—then we walked quietly to a room on the floor below to plan what was next for the team and for us.

We closed the door and decided that first things first we were going to vent. And we did—until we got it out of our systems and were able to put on a good face and not create any unnecessary concerns. Then we headed to meet the team together and started a super-transparent communication process and a restructuring. Prab, who had been my peer, became my boss as well as my partner in managing change. This is his philosophy on starting from scratch.

"Today, there are fewer and fewer situations where people stay in a career for a long period, and we need to get comfortable making sudden or frequent changes. This means career management is now a job. What I experience is that people reactively manage their careers. Something happened at your job, so you look for your next thing; your boss says something wrong, and you react by looking for a new job. Today you need to be proactive, but not many are wired this way and lack the necessary confidence to constantly shop around. I see people with little experience but big egos and lots of followers doing well because they shop a lot. The average person doesn't have that, and they become a needle in the haystack. "

. . . .

Now that we've looked at some ways to build resilience, it's time to put them into practice with this chapter's homework.

Developing Your Resilience

Think about the four areas where you can develop resilience and one thing in each area that you can do to improve.

1. How connected are you to family, friends, and colleagues? What is one thing you can do to strengthen or expand those connections? Write it here:

Family: _____

Friends: _____

Current or ex-colleagues: _____

(If you need some inspiration, look at https://www.gratitude-andpasta.com/ or look for one of Chris Schembra's videos that help unpack human connections.)

2. Are you taking care of yourself physically, mentally, and emotionally? What one thing can you add to or change about your routine that will make you stronger? As an "always on" person, I will not tell you to meditate or do yoga if it's not your thing. I really wished it was mine, but there are great free or affordable apps like Calm, Headspace, and others that can help. I use a deep-focus music playlist on YouTube or Spotify and close my eyes, or I take a walk listening to it at a volume that would not be out of place in a club in Vegas—I find it doesn't let any other thoughts in my head and supports my unwinding. Whatever you choose, let's have you commit and write it here:

_____

3. What gives you purpose in life? Now is the time to add something to your day that gives you purpose. If there's a specific cause or group you care about, try volunteering for that cause just one time and see how it feels. Or maybe your purpose is reaching a personal goal. Whatever will bring some purpose into your life, write down here what that thing will be:

_____

_____

_____

4. How is your mindset? To make sure you're thinking healthy thoughts and focusing on the positive, write down things in your life that you're grateful for here. If you struggle, that's OK. Make sure you reframe any negative thoughts with this question: "What would I tell a friend who had this thought?"

_____

_____

_____

_____

Consider using a daily journal for building this muscle. I like https://www.intelligentchange.com/journals (for my kids too!), but if you just google "gratitude journals," you'll discover many great ones.

In the next chapter, we'll cover what other things you can do to always be ready to start from scratch. Unlike the other chapters that focus on you, this time we will focus on others.

CHAPTER 3:

Build Your Personal Board of Directors

···

"If you are successful, it is because somewhere, sometime, someone gave you a life or an idea that started you in the right direction."
—MELINDA FRENCH GATES

No one ever becomes a success in a vacuum. We need other people, whether it's to supervise our work, bounce ideas off, help us get things done, recognize our successes, or guide us through the rough patches of work and life. Having a network you can rely on is always important; however, when it comes to starting from scratch, it's crucial. The people around you, at your company and in your field, can be a tremendous source of inspiration, information, advice, and support. They can help you make the ultimate decision as to whether you need to start from scratch as well as where to do it and how. And once you do, they can help you prepare for the next phase of your life.

You may already have some form of board of directors in your life right now, especially if you've been in the workforce for a while. You've probably gathered a network of current and former coworkers, bosses, colleagues, mentors, even employees. In this chapter, I'm going to help you look to that network and beyond it to assemble a team of people you can turn to when you need guidance or support that's specific and steady—the kind of guidance you need when you're starting from scratch.

We're going to build your personal board of directors, or PBOD.

Your PBOD is a group of people you enlist to support you, mentor you, help you find things you need, teach you things, help you solve problems, give you honest advice, and update you on the latest information in your company, the company you hope to work for in the future, and your field. And that's just a partial list.

Some people tend to look to their close circle of friends or family for this kind of support, but that is very much *not* what I'm talking about here. The whole point of these relationships is that these people are *neutral*—they can look at whatever question or problem you bring to them with complete detachment from the outcome. Your friends and family can certainly offer their help, but they cannot take the place of a person with no emotional investment. Therefore, it is important to get out of your comfort zone and curate and create relationships of trust, learning, and inspiration with people who are not your friends but are still open enough to support your growth. These are people whom you bring into your life, or relationships you nurture, for the specific purpose of obtaining advice, inspiration, and/ or support. Sometimes you even need them to give you tough love.

It's a unique kind of relationship, which is why it gets an entire chapter in this book.

Because these people are neutral, they can provide the right kind of support you need when you're starting from scratch. They can help you see the things you don't see and do the things you don't know how to do. They can help you decide if you're on the right path, validate your ideas, even just care about you when you need to feel like there's someone in your corner.

I'm not saying your family and friends can't be a part of your support network. My family is my world, and my husband is probably the most important supporter I have. And the support he offers me is excellent. He knows me really well, especially after working through a pandemic from the same New York City apartment. Sometimes he'll say something relevant to something I'm going through. I'll look at him and ask, "How did you know that?" He'll always say, "I can hear you talk. I listen." I consult with him a lot, because I respect his opinion, and he does know how to give me both regular love and tough love. But when I'm starting from scratch, I (and you) need something more.

Why Do You Need a PBOD?

You need a personal board of directors for the same reason you don't always listen to your husband … or your mother. Sometimes you need someone outside your circle to look at a situation objectively. Sometimes you need someone to tell you what you *need* to hear as opposed to what you *want* to hear. You need a person with some distance who won't be affected by the outcome or your feelings about their suggestions or comments.

> **Sometimes you need someone to tell you what you need to hear as opposed to what you want to hear.**

At other times—and this is probably more common—you need someone that understands something specific about your profession, or the organizational climate, or your role. While you can involve anyone you want in your PBOD for any purpose, it's crucial to have some people who really understand the ins and outs of your industry.

According to Forbes Council of Coaches member Lisa Barrington, "Your PBOD exists to act as a sounding board, to advise you, and to provide you with feedback on your life decisions, opportunities, and challenges. They provide you with unfiltered feedback that you can't necessarily get from colleagues or friends."[11]

I'm not suggesting you need to formally invite all these people to "serve" on your board. Not everyone on my PBOD even knows they're on my PBOD or that I have one at all. Some do and some don't. But while they're not my best friends at work or in my field (and don't need to be), they do share some general qualities. They tend to be people I enjoy for one reason or another. Something happens to my brain, or sometimes my soul, when I am with them. That's actually a good description of why you need a PBOD: to help take your brain and/or soul places they might not ordinarily go. To look at an issue in your life or career with a fresh pair of eyes and a perspective that's different from yours and from that of the people you usually surround yourself with. Arnaud Collery, in his book *Mister Happiness*, calls them "angels." I like it, but when I meet people who tell me they don't know who is or can be on their PBOD, I say, "Close your eyes, and imagine you're walking down a path toward your goal. Who is there smiling, clapping, worried? Who walks next to you? Who walks behind you so you don't fall or in front of you to guide the way? Those people are on your PBOD."

. . . .

Jonaed Iqbal has more than 36,000 followers on LinkedIn at the time of writing this! Yes, he is the founder of NoDegree.com and a podcaster (among a long list of other talents), but actually, he attributes his popularity to always being a networker.

---

11   Lisa Barrington, "Everyone Needs a Personal Board of Directors," *Forbes*, February 20, 2018, https://www.forbes.com/sites/forbescoachescouncil/2018/02/20/everyone-needs-a-personal-board-of-directors/?sh=289b5fb42bbc.

As he has such a vast number of followers, I was interested in whether Jonaed had a PBOD. He explained that in his view, networking needs to focus on helping others: "Be intentional, strategic, and willing to help others, and seeds will be planted for them to give back when you need them as well." Jonaed recalled multiple instances when people gave him advice or even offered their services for free because he had supported them in the past. "They saw my action to share good advice, make an introduction, or help them with something more technical as if I invested in their success, so when I need help, they are always there for me too."

How does he suggest building your own PBOD? "Don't reach out when you need something. Build a relationship first, listen to one's story. If they helped you, ask how you can be of help as well. It doesn't need to happen immediately, but stay in touch.

"Being an introvert doesn't mean you aren't friendly or lack social skills to network. It just means that it takes more energy from yourself to network, and that's okay, so start with closer friend circles.

"Cold outreach isn't always awkward, and sometimes the other side appreciates it and doesn't think you are awkward—don't overjudge yourself. Still, don't make cold outreach 'too cold.' Be smart, and research the person. Start on LinkedIn. If they write a blog, read it; if they have a podcast, listen to it. People will be excited to get on a call with you if your interest is genuine.

"Build your community. Whatever your interests or hobbies are, there are plenty of clubs, groups, and people to follow on Twitter or Discord to connect and learn from. Having a mutual interest is an easy first way to start connecting ."

How to Build Your Board

I'm definitely not the first person to suggest creating some sort of informal personal advisory board. It's becoming common business practice—and it's really just a targeted, specific kind of networking. It's networking with purpose. So how, short of sending out a formal invitation, should you assemble your own personal team of avengers? *Fast Company* advises readers to build what they call a "Personal Board of Advisors" by seeking "relationships with different people who can provide insight based on their various skills and backgrounds … similar to what a business would seek in their corporate board members." They also helpfully suggest people who fit into one or more of the following categories:

- ⮕ Industry expert

- ⮕ Strong supporter

- ⮕ Thoughtful critic

- ⮕ Networker[12]

That's a really good start, but you definitely want more than four people on your board. *Forbes* is a little more specific with its suggestions, advising you to look for the following:

- ⮕ Someone in your field (e.g., in your profession or industry)

- ⮕ Someone who is in or has been in your circumstance (e.g., immigrant, parent, single parent, transitioning careers later in life)

- ⮕ Someone who is one of your greatest cheerleaders

---

12 Jeff Berger, "Why Every Professional Should Recruit a Personal Board of Advisors," *Fast Company*, February 17, 2020, https://www.fastcompany.com/90464678/why-every-professional-should-recruit-a-personal-board-of-advisors.

➔ Someone who has and is ready to critique you (your decisions/actions)

➔ Someone who is a leader in the area in which you aspire to grow or succeed (e.g., professional, spiritual, personal)

➔ Someone of another generation (one person from a generation older and one person from a generation younger)

➔ Someone who can introduce you to others (e.g., in your profession or community)[13]

Find good people you trust to fill each of these roles (knowingly or not), and you will have the beginnings of an excellent PBOD. Try to keep a balance—you're looking for people who will deliver the brutal, honest truth when you need it, but you're also looking for people who make you feel good. At least some members of your PBOD should be people who can pick you up when you're down, celebrate with you, and also inspire you.

Someone who fits this category is a woman I once interviewed for a job. She really wanted to work for me, but I got a sense that at the end of the day what she *really* wanted to do was start her own company. And my sense was that if she did that, even if she failed, she would learn and grow and get where she wanted to go much faster than she would by working for me. Not that I wouldn't have wanted her to work for me—I loved her! I just didn't think it would be the right thing for her, which ultimately would make it the wrong thing for me.

After I interviewed this woman, I assumed she'd just fade into the sort of jumble of the hundreds of people I've met over the years of

---

13   Lisa Barrington, "Everyone Needs a Personal Board of Directors," Forbes, Feb. 20, 2018, https://www.forbes.com/sites/forbescoachescouncil/2018/02/20/everyone-needs-a-personal-board-of-directors/?sh=61111def2bbc.

my career. I thought maybe she'd start that company, and maybe she'd pop up on my radar someday down the line. So I was really surprised when she sent me an email telling me she was adding me to a special list she'd compiled of a hundred people who inspired her. Every year, she sends each person on that list an email talking about what she'd accomplished that year in a really honest, straightforward, not-at-all-braggy way. It was strange—I didn't know her that well, but thanks to that email, she suddenly became interesting to me. And today, I still care about what she's working on, and her success, because of the way she is sharing it with the world.

. . . .

Sometimes, a person on your PBOD believes in you more than you believe in yourself. They might see something in you that you can't even fathom you can do. Hilla Bakshi learned this firsthand.

Hilla recalls "losing herself" in 2016. She had just returned from a relocation job in San Francisco and couldn't decide what she wanted to do or be. She joined several Facebook groups for women and started attending meetups. "I remember going to these events and seeing people that became my role models."

One day her manager told her she must start doing something with all the information she gathered at those meetups. She became this "woman who goes to meetups"—that go-to person whom everyone knows is the one to ask when they're looking for a good meetup for a particular purpose. In fact, she had a note on her iPhone with the email addresses of people she should contact when going to specific events.

After some needs analysis, she started her own Facebook group and named it HaMeetupistiot ("women who go to meetups" in

Hebrew). The need was so present that she had five hundred women registered in two weeks. Her agenda was clear. She wanted to build a community for women that elevated women and brought them to meetups not just as attendees but as speakers, panelists, and representatives. She wanted to build a safe space where women could write, consult, and ask questions freely. She made each attendee a brand on their own and created "the spotlight," where she featured someone from the community and told their story. Other attendees started summarizing meetup takeaways, and slowly but surely, the community grew large and robust.

Hilla says the women on her PBOD are also her role models, women of whom she says, "When I grow up, I want to be like them." She has a colleague who is her North Star, whom she admires but also supports. Another woman she admires serves as her coach, but she supports her by building her brand. Because, as you'll see over and over again in this book, the best PBOD is one that is reciprocal, where everyone gets something out of it.

Know Your Types

Ultimately, I like to look for people who can bring out the creativity in me, or help me make better decisions, or offer a reality check, or even provide a certain something I can't put my finger on that just makes me better. Your specific requirements will be different, but those are the kinds of feelings these people should evoke in you. Ideally, at least one of them will work within your organization, so they will be familiar with your day-to-day environment, the people you need to deal with, and the other challenges you face. I have some PBOD members who are currently external to the organization where I work but who worked there in the past, so they understand the lay of the land to some degree. Other members include former bosses, former colleagues, and people I've met through the course of my career.

A PBOD member can be someone who is your peer, or someone who is more senior to you. A lot of times I rely on my peers—usually a certain type of peer who is not too close to me but I either love *what* they do or I love *how* they do it. The people who make me think, *Damn, I wish I'd thought of that.* They make me want to be as good as they are. That's what I mean by inspiring. I really value the perspective of people who do things differently than I do and have different strengths and gifts. When the way someone does something is different from your way, it teaches you something—it stretches your capacity because it can open you up to different ways of doing things.

I also choose my board members with an eye to including a variety of types of people, because I want individuals who will serve different purposes. Some are there for creative inspiration while others help with more interpersonal issues. One will give me more tough love, and another will always remind me how amazing I am. Which reminds me—*don't* just stack your PBOD with a bunch of people who think you're amazing. Not that you aren't amazing, but having a couple of PBOD members who will give you the bad news is really, really important. You need somebody to keep you grounded and also someone who pushes you, even when you don't want to be pushed. Although I do have a board member who reminds me of how amazing I am every time I speak to them. Sometimes you need that too. But there are other members on my board who, while I'm sure they very much appreciate me, would probably not waste their time lavishing me with praise.

Ultimately, I think you calibrate what you need for your particular situation and personality and then find people to fill those roles whose opinions or presence or perspective you value greatly. For example, in my previous role, we had a chief marketing officer who was much more senior than me. She presented her work and came up with an idea for a new brand, which is what CMOs do, so for her it wasn't anything special. But for me it was inspiring. This CMO briefly involved me in her research, interviewing me as one of the people who should have an opinion about what she was doing, and it really impressed me. The interview process was so different than what I'd expected—it was thoughtful, it was creative, and it was engaging. I've been working with marketing people for many, many years, usually as peers, but this experience was totally different.

I was so impressed that I approached her after our meeting and told her so. I also asked her if she would mind walking me through her thought process so I could understand how this brilliant, inspiring *thing* had come together. So, she did. And as we talked, our conversation sparked a question about my own job. I was having an issue explaining something to our customers, so I asked her, "How would you deliver this message?" Her answer really helped me, and I think she understood that when she offered it, it meant something to me.

That was the beginning of her stint as a member of my PBOD.

Not that I came right out and asked her, "Would you join my personal board of directors?" She might have looked at me like I was crazy. But I did ask, "Will it be okay for me to come see you again in the future?" She said yes, and so, from time to time, I would. I would follow up, or I would come by to say hi, or I would just send a note: "I was just thinking about ..." "I saw something that you did," "I saw someone on your team, and it was great. And thanks again." Basically, I nurtured the relationship, but not in a stalker-y way. She was more senior than me, and I respected that; I respected her time, and I respected the fact she gave *me* time.

Nurturing a relationship doesn't have to be complicated. Touch base occasionally to let someone know you care, that you're thinking about them. Like how I send one of my ex-bosses a text every St. Patrick's Day because he's Irish, and he comes back with a text every Mother's Day because I'm a mom. It's a gesture that we've adopted to ping each other between the times we talk or catch up in real life.

Nurturing a relationship can mean sustaining a relationship, but it can also mean growing one. That happened with the senior marketing woman I mentioned above. For a long time, everything I asked her was very much in her wheelhouse, since we weren't in the same line of work. However, over time I wound up valuing her perspective so much that I decided to consult with her about things that were more personal to my role, to see if she could help me in other areas. She became a really important voice in my professional life.

I think she understood that I had kind of adopted her, but I never officially said, "This is my mentor." I usually reserve that for people who I pay for specific types of help or coaching, not people whom I turn to for advice and support. I keep it informal so there's no pressure or expectation on them.

For example, one member of my board is one of my previous bosses. And whenever I contact him, it still feels very much like I'm calling my previous boss. He's still very formal with me, to the point where he gives me feedback and his perspective in the same way he would have delivered my performance review! It's not always a lot of fun, but sometimes I need that. Sometimes I feel like maybe I'm derailing, or maybe I'm not sure about my choices, and sometimes I need his honest perspective. So he's my reality check person.

Everyone needs a reality check person, because it's easy to get so caught up in what you're doing that you miss important signs and signals. For example, when I feel like everything is great and work is humming along with no drama, I tend to worry that maybe I'm not seeing the whole picture. That's when I'll turn to him. Before I joined WeWork, I also asked for his opinion. Everyone I knew was pushing me to take the job, saying, "Are you joking? How are you even debating joining this amazing company?" But I wasn't 100 percent sure. I'd been through so much drama and started from scratch so many times that I wanted to be careful, especially about a company with so much crazy energy swirling around it. Plus, I wasn't sure it was positioning its focus as a tech company, and I didn't want to work for a non-tech company.

But everybody around me thought I was nuts for even thinking twice. To the point where I had several people telling me, "I would work there for free."

I deliberated so long, WeWork actually raised its offer. But I still couldn't decide. That's when I realized I needed a reality check, and that's when I contacted my old boss and explained the situation. I asked him, "What do you think? Am I crazy? I only hear good things about this company, so why do I debate it? What is happening?" Thankfully, he was a little more circumspect about the whole idea of WeWork. He said, "Listen, it's super interesting what is happening to this company. Why everybody's so crazed about it, I don't understand. But that doesn't mean anything. All that matters is this: *What is your job? What do you want to do? What will working there teach you?*

Those three questions brought me back down to earth. They helped me cut through all the noise and hype around WeWork and focus on reality, which was what my actual job would be at the micro level, day to day. Would it be good? Would it be interesting? Would I grow? Would it be different from what I was currently doing? When I looked at it from that perspective, I realized that the job checked all my boxes, and I was able to make a decision. So, I wound up taking it, but thanks to this one member of my PBOD, I took the job feeling confident that I was taking it for the right reasons. And despite all the craziness that went on within the company, it turned out to be a great growth and learning experience for me.

· ·

I came across this post from Melissa Cohen, founder and owner of MBC Consulting Solutions, that details the right way to build your own PBOD.

> *I love networking. Nearly every opportunity I have ever had came from someone within my network. Your network is one of the most valuable assets you will ever have.*
>
> *The year 2022 seems to have awakened something in people, as my inbox and DMs are being inundated with requests. I have met some incredibly interesting people and reconnected with friends and former colleagues.*
>
> *If I might be so bold, I would like to make some suggestions for reaching out on LinkedIn.*
>
> ⊙ *If we don't already know each other, err on the side of professionalism. I do not need to be (nor want to be) greeted with "Dear Mrs. Cohen," but I would prefer not to get a "Hey, Mel." I hate the nickname Mel. No one in their life has ever called me Mel and gotten away with it.*
>
> ⊙ *Please don't start off with a sales pitch before we have even connected. If I don't know you, the likelihood of my paying for your services right out of the gate is pretty close to zero.*
>
> ⊙ *Someone who I admire very much, Susan Collins, PHR, CI, has the quote "Give more than you get" in her tagline.*

This always resonated with me. I love to help people (most people do). But help is a two-way street. If you are asking for something, offer something in return. I met with an extremely impressive young woman this morning who wanted to ask me a few questions and hear about my career trajectory. She had taken the time to read some of my posts and knew what I was interested in. She sent me some wonderful podcast links on NFTs. I definitely feel that I got the better end of the deal!

⊙ *Keep in regular communication. We are all incredibly busy, but if the only time I hear from you is when you need a reference, or are looking for a job and want help getting a foot in the door, that's not networking. Comment on your connections' posts. Send them articles that you think they would find of interest. Send them a message or email just to say you're thinking of them, or on a milestone (birthday, holiday). When you do meet (virtually or otherwise), exchange ideas and ask what you can be of help with.*

In other words, try to make sure there's something in it for them, too. The strongest relationships are always reciprocal.

Don't Be Shy

I get that not everyone is an extrovert (I definitely am not), and the idea of reaching out to an ex-boss or someone you look up to and asking them for help may sound scary. I promise you, it doesn't need to be. As I already mentioned, where my PBOD is concerned, some of them know they're my advisors and some absolutely don't. However,

I think it's more than okay to reach out to someone on LinkedIn and say, "Hi, your job is really interesting to me, and I'm curious to learn more. Would you mind spending fifteen minutes with me?" If you're not coming across like you're trying to sell them something, most people will be happy to help.

I had someone reach out to me in this way. She had listened to a podcast that I was on and had actually written questions down, in part because she disagreed with some of the stuff that I'd said! She shared her own thinking process with me and added that she would love to debate me. I was so impressed. I thought, *Wow, she really listened. She gave it thought.* She did her homework and did everything she could without me and was just asking for fifteen minutes of my time. How could I say no?

Not that you should always expect people to be available. Everybody's busy. So you need to choose your time and how you spend your time, and of course be strategic about how you ask. Remember, it can also be in writing. Not everyone is available for a call. But when someone approaches me the way this person did, adding the fact that she did her homework and listened and had an opinion about something that I'd said, I felt that took her to the next level. She was definitely worth an investment of my time.

I don't know if she considers me a part of her PBOD. But I would be honored if she does.

Let's Build a Personal Board of Directors

Being ready to start from scratch means having your PBOD in place so you can mine them for information, get their expert advice, lean on them for support when you need it, and get a reality check when you need that. So now is the time to start thinking about the people in your life, especially your professional life, who can give you the perspective, support, reality check, or whatever else you might need to successfully start from scratch.

Think about the types of people you need for your PBOD. Do you need someone to inspire you? Someone to tell you you're amazing? Someone to kick your butt a little? Someone to fill you in on what you don't know? Write down all the roles that you imagine need to be filled. If you need some inspiration, start with that *Forbes* list I mentioned earlier. Here's a reminder:

➲ Someone in your field (e.g., in your profession or industry)

➲ Someone who is in or has been in your circumstance (e.g., parent, single parent, transitioning careers later in life)

➲ Someone who is one of your greatest cheerleaders

➲ Someone who has and is ready to critique you (your decisions/ actions)

➲ Someone who is a leader in the area in which you aspire to grow or succeed (e.g., professional, spiritual, personal)

➔ Someone of another generation (one person from a generation older and one person from a generation younger)

➔ Someone who can introduce you to others (e.g., in your profession or community)

Now, think about the people you know who might best fill those roles. Whom do you know who is so great at what they do that you're actually jealous? Who will tell you you're amazing when you need to hear it? Who will give you bad news when you need to hear that? Who knows everyone in your industry and is on top of all the latest comings and goings? Who approaches problems in a way you think is impressive? Who just makes you feel good?

Think about the people you know who inspire you, who make you think, who help you expand your perspective, and who just generally make you better. Then, when you've found the perfect person, write their name down next to the role.

EXAMPLE 1:

ROLE: Someone in your field

....

NAME: Sara Smith

....

REACH-OUT METHOD:

She just posted an interesting post on LinkedIn. Will support her by commenting on it and ask to reconnect.

EXAMPLE 2:

ROLE: Someone who has and is ready to critique you

NAME: Joe Carry

REACH-OUT METHOD:

Will send an email mentioning that I remember their feedback and hope they are well and offer to meet online or over coffee.

ROLE:

NAME:

REACH-OUT METHOD:

ROLE:

NAME:

REACH-OUT METHOD:

ROLE:

NAME:

REACH-OUT METHOD:

ROLE:

NAME:

REACH-OUT METHOD:

ROLE:

NAME:

REACH-OUT METHOD:

ROLE:

NAME:

REACH-OUT METHOD:

ROLE:

NAME:

REACH-OUT METHOD:

ROLE:

NAME:

REACH-OUT METHOD:

Now it's time for step two: reaching out to the people on your list. You don't have to officially ask them to be on your PBOD—they might think that's a little presumptuous, depending on how senior they are to you. The idea is to start a dialogue. Let them know why they inspire you, especially if you can remember a specific instance you can refer to. Congratulate them on an accomplishment or milestone, or comment on an article or podcast of theirs. Tell them you value their opinion, and ask their advice. And start cultivating the relationships that will help you build a strong PBOD to guide you through what's coming next.

We'll look at that "what's coming next" in the next chapter, when we explore what I call "the spark."

CHAPTER 4:

The Spark

....

After surviving several reorgs, I've learned to spot the signs that change is coming. Something happens, and something else happens, and my Spidey sense starts to tingle. I feel the change in the air. Something definitely feels off.

I call it the spark, because it's the beginning of something, the way a spark starts a fire. You feel the spark because you know on some level that something is happening, even if you can't put your finger on exactly what it is. All you know is that when and if that something happens, you will very likely have to start from scratch.

A spark is both the sense that problems and/or opportunities are on the horizon and a warning to get yourself ready for what's coming. And it doesn't have to be scary if you know how to make the most of it. This chapter will show you how.

There are actually two kinds of sparks, and while they share some similarities, they're two very different animals.

External sparks are when something happens *to* you that lets you know you might need to start from scratch soon. They can involve the company you work for, but they can also happen in a personal context—signs that a partner is losing interest, that your health might not be optimal, that something about your circumstances is about to change can all be sparks. But for now, let's concentrate on sparks in a professional context.

At work, an external spark can be something company specific, like the following:

- ➔ Your company acquiring or being acquired by another company

- ➔ A change in the marketplace or new development affecting the industry your company is in

- ➔ The result of a funding round or IPO

Or it can be people specific, like the following:

- ➔ A reorg or change in management

- ➔ A peer's or your boss's promotion or departure

- ➔ A new person being added to your team

All these events, as well as many more that I haven't listed here, are sparks that indicate a change is coming, and you will likely have to deal with it in one way or another. Paying attention to these sparks early and taking action based on the information you take in leaves you better prepared to make the most of any opportunities that arise from the situation or to prepare yourself to deal with the fallout. Either way, it's about staying on top of the situation so that whatever happens, you aren't caught off guard and are able to make the most of it and start from scratch on your own terms.

Internal sparks are when something happens *inside* you that might mean it's time to consider starting from scratch. Nothing new or different may be going on with your company or your life, but maybe you feel a sense of dissatisfaction or unease, or even excitement and interest in something different. Professionally, an internal spark might feel something like the following:

⊛ You feel limited in your job.

⊛ You don't enjoy the relationships with the people you work with.

⊛ You feel like you've completed the work that you were hired to do.

⊛ You have another interest you've always wanted to pursue, and it feels like time is running out.

⊛ You're intrigued by an opportunity that will take you in another direction.

⊛ You're burned out and ready to try something new.

In a personal context, you might feel stifled in a relationship, or you might decide you hate living where you live, or you might feel motivated to take control of your health. What's important to recognize is that these kinds of feelings are sparks, just like external sparks. The only difference is, they're hints that come from your own subconscious (or conscious) mind. Those hints tell you that even though the circumstances in your life might not demand it, it might be time to get ready to start from scratch because it might be the right move for you. Paying attention to those sparks early and dealing with them in a systematic,

External and internal sparks are different in origin, but they ultimately serve the same purpose. They're both early indicators that it's time to get yourself and your stuff in order.

step-by-step way can help you decide when to hold off, when it's right to make a change, and how to do it while burning as few bridges as possible and laying the groundwork for success and growth.

External and internal sparks are different in origin, but they ultimately serve the same purpose. They're both early indicators that it's time to get yourself and your stuff in order. If you've been doing the work over the last three chapters, things should be pretty close to lined up. If not, you know how to put the pieces in place so you'll be ready to make your move when the time is right.

. . . .

Maria Rosati believes that the old rules we were taught about staying in the same role or with the same company throughout our career no longer work. "We are all living longer and may have several careers," she explains. "As an active member of Chief, the private network for female executives, I see it all the time. We are all in some sort of career transformation."

In her last corporate role, Maria worked for eleven and a half years in corporate communications for a financial firm. She constantly felt like she was a cog in the wheel. "I was walking around work with a feeling that they would be totally okay with or without me. It's not personal; I was just keeping the machine going but did not have an overwhelming sense of purpose." That realization was the spark to take back control of her career path.

Maria realized she needed to make moves and not wait for things to happen to her. "I knew it was just a matter of time before I left the company. As an eternal optimist, I spent the last two years of my corporate career plotting my next move. I spent a lot of time networking, talking to vendors, and learning about the latest industry trends and best practices so that once I left, I had a road map for my future. I took control of what was to come."

This kind of thinking is important today more than ever.

"Most large corporations, especially public companies, spend a lot of time reorganizing to meet financial goals and deliver value to shareholders. What they don't do is deliver value for the employees. I believe that is what the 'Great Resignation' is all about."

Maria chose not to get another corporate job. She knew she would be pigeonholed into another corporate communications role, which she had already determined was too narrow in scope for her. She also looked around and did not see many women over age sixty in senior roles in communications. But instead of panicking about her prospects, "I saw this as an opportunity," Maria explains. "I felt it was my chance: I either put in three years and reinvent myself in a new organization but be pushed out because of my high compensation, or I spend the same amount of time on starting my own company, which I could run for the next twenty years."

Maria credits her success to being agile and able to constantly pivot. "Choosing the next door you open," is how she puts it. In fact, she believes that staying in the same role for a long period of time leads to stagnation. "You stop learning and just become a cog in the machine." By starting from scratch when she felt the spark, Maria built her own machine.

. . . .

Responding to External Sparks

Back when I was at AOL, after the company was acquired by Verizon, there were a lot of rumors about our team. Were we duplicated with another team? Did Verizon need both teams going forward? There were a lot of politics around who was going to lead. And while I felt accomplished in my role, I didn't feel like whatever was coming for me personally was going to be something bigger or better.

I didn't feel the way I later felt at WeWork, when the assumption was that we were going to go public and therefore would have more money and more attention. This wasn't a new start-up company; it was Verizon. The business was very mature. My role was very mature. And while I had a very big team, the question that nagged at me was this: *Is there anything more to be done here?* It didn't feel like we had bigger, better plans on the horizon. Especially with conversations happening all around us saying that someone else was doing the same work and we were basically being evaluated in the following terms: *What's redundant? What's better? Who's going to lead the team?*

Those questions, the fact that we had been acquired, and the general sense that our work was not particularly appreciated or measured in the same manner were all (external) sparks for me. Those sparks meant my situation might change, and I might have to start from scratch. So, my goal became to do what I could to control what form that restart would take as much as I possibly could.

My initial sense was that a lot of my stakeholders and my part of the organization weren't being included in the right conversations (including myself). So I thought, *Okay, this is not going in a good direction. Is there something better here?*

I started looking around within the company for other opportunities. What's really nice about big organizations like Verizon is that they support internal mobility. There's usually either a process or a person who you can talk to, and it's safe—your job is not at risk just because you're looking around, because you're looking within the organization. It's not like you're "cheating" on your boss. So, I started looking around and speaking to other people at Verizon. I didn't see anything that was relevant to me or a specific job that I wanted, but I did decide who I wanted to work for.

I wanted to work for the company CTO.

It was far-fetched. The CTO didn't have any people in my position reporting to him. But I was determined that the man would be my boss. And I did wind up working for him—not because there was a role for me but because I built a role for myself, as I explained in a previous chapter. In the context of this chapter, what's important is that I paid attention to the sparks, avoided being made redundant, and actually created the job I wanted working for the person I wanted to work for. I had engineered my own happy ending ...

... except, as so often happens in tech, the story wasn't over.

A year after I moved into the job I created for myself, Verizon bought another company, which threw everything into flux again. Even though I was in execution mode and getting used to the new role I had created, a year later there were too many rumors flying around about big changes coming within the organization for me to get complacent. After all, those rumors were also (external) sparks, and I needed to pay attention and come up with a plan—especially because I knew my new boss was now at flight risk. This was no time to put my execution-mode blinders on. I might have to start from scratch yet again.

My boss was very well regarded, and everybody thought highly of him. I wasn't the only person who wanted to work with him, so I never really thought that, between him and his potential replacement, he wouldn't win the battle and keep his job. However, I still had a plan B. After all, with the new acquisition, who knew what might be on the horizon? Maybe more opportunities were about to open. Maybe there would be a bigger role for me. And maybe, despite how well liked my boss was, he would still lose or leave.

In that case, the other company's CEO was also very well regarded, and additionally, she happened to be known as one of the top product management leaders in the world. So even though I liked my boss so much that I had gone through the trouble of creating my own job just to work for him, I also saw the possibility of working for this woman as an opportunity I couldn't pass up. And either way, it didn't really matter. The external sparks were there; some kind of change was on the horizon, and I needed to prepare to start from scratch no matter what happened next. So I needed to find a way to get on this woman's radar.

Because of her high profile, this CEO had a really strong management team around her. I knew it would be really difficult to infiltrate that team. So, I tackled it step by step. First, I learned everything there was to know about their organization. Then I started speaking to other people about it. I did a lot of research to try to see if there was another avenue in. If I couldn't get accepted to work for my dream boss, could I come pitch her an idea?

The answer turned out to be none of the above. My then-current boss lost the contest and had to leave the company. And my dream boss decided she didn't want the job and also left.

So I did, in fact, need to start from scratch yet again. The sparks didn't lie.

But I was ready. I was already in that mindset: *Okay, I'm looking, I'm preparing myself, and I'm polishing myself.* So I was ready for whatever came next.

In fact, when both my new boss and my potential new boss left, because I had responded to the sparks, I actually had four other opportunities in the company. One of them was facilitated by my ex-boss, who spoke on my behalf to a team that I thought would be amazing to work for. HR brought another opportunity to me, and I was building two others on my own through socializing and researching.

I wound up taking the opportunity that my ex-boss recommended I take, which was something outside product management in a completely new direction—a direction that turned out to be totally wrong for me. Which leads me to the other kind of spark ...

Responding to Internal Sparks

Two weeks into my job, I knew I had made a terrible mistake. My internal sparks were going off like a fire alarm. But the question quickly turned from *Oh no, what did I do?* to *How long do I need to stay here to maintain my brand internally and not ruin the relationship?* I was working for one of the strongest leaders not only in the city but probably in the industry. So if I jumped ship, if someone asked her about me, she might say, "Well, she's good, but she hasn't completed what I needed her to do. Maybe she's good, but she hasn't done too much with us, so I don't know. I can't recommend her."

That's when I had to say, "Okay, this role is not for me. And maybe there are other opportunities. But the price of jumping ship now would be too high."

So how long would I actually need to stay?

Am I Done?

Before moving on from a role, I determine what I need to accomplish to be able to say, "I finished; I'm done"—and in this case, so that my new boss would agree that I was finished and give me the blessing to go. This is something I have done ever since my very first job. Which I got accidentally. Which is a whole other story.

When I applied for my first job, I actually knew the people and the company that was hiring. They had been a client of a company I'd worked for when I was in college, and I knew they thought highly of me. But when I saw the job was available (in the newspaper—this was a long time ago!), I applied the old-fashioned way. I filled out an application and sent my CV in the mail. Snail mail. Which would make it the equivalent of applying to work at a company where you knew the owner through a job posting on LinkedIn or Indeed today. I applied blind.

However, I did do one thing beyond the basics. I wanted a way for my CV to stick out, so I contacted a friend who designed it for me, and then I printed it on colored paper.

And it definitely stuck out, because not long after I sent my CV in, the company HR contacted me and asked, "Is this you?" I told them it was. And they said, "What were you thinking? Why didn't you just come and tell us that you wanted the job?"

It was true. I knew them. I knew them very well. But it never occurred to me to use that fact to try to get a job with them. I thought that would be weird. Or even unethical. Like I was taking unfair advantage. (Remember, this was my first job, and I was very young ...)

The person who called me said, "Okay, so here's the thing. The job is closed. It was taken." At the time, this was a very small company with only about thirty people, although it's a huge public company today. "But," they went on, "the CEO wants to speak to you." So I met with him. It wasn't an interview. It was an open conversation because the role was taken; there was no job to be discussed.

I spoke to him at length, and we had a great conversation. I felt like this guy could actually mentor me to my next job, because he was full of ideas. I felt very grown up, like it was my first "in the adult working world" kind of situation. Plus, the way he asked me questions, trying to learn about me, I thought, *Wow. I like this person.* Maybe this was because his questions had the odd effect of getting me to say more good things about myself than I actually remembered, or knew, or could admit.

When we ended the conversation, he said, "So listen—I feel like you could do a lot of things here in the company. But I actually want you to get that job you applied for, not the other person. We'll find him another role—I want you for this job. But first, what I want you to tell me is this: When do you think you'll be done?"

That was a mentoring moment.

When would I be done? What did he mean?

It was a very hard question to answer. I had never done this job before. I had never done any "real" job before, outside of jobs I'd had when I was in high school and in college. So I needed to put a picture of myself doing this job in my head. Then I could figure out the following:

→ This is what I can accomplish in the job.

→ This is what would take regular expectations to the next level of execution.

→ This is when I'll actually be done doing the job.

As a student, I had worked for this man's company as a tutor for executives, teaching them how to move to the new Windows and Office programs (this was back in the year 2000). In the role he wanted to hire me for, I was supposed to build a whole educational department for the company. After thinking it through, I told him, "I'll be done when I have multiple schools around the world, and they'll all have signs on the door."

How did I come up with that? Well, I hadn't learned the job because the job was new, but I did understand that it was a global company. So I knew I would need to open offices around the world. I would need to hire people to work in those offices. I would need to create a curriculum that all the offices would use. And then I figured we would just replicate it—office by office, by office, by office. And, of course, they would all have signs on the door.

Like I said, I was really, really, *really* young.

Five years later, we opened the London office. I went to the UK for the opening. I had a manager there, I had a team there, and we did our first class there. And when I closed the door and I saw the sign, it hit me.

I was done.

Now, I had closed other doors with other signs on them before. I'd opened offices in New York and New Jersey and Germany and Tel Aviv, among others. But I never felt that "Okay, I'm done" moment until London. Because that was when I realized there was nothing more for me to do other than the sixth, the seventh, the eighth … and the company didn't really need me for those. I had built a system that was working.

From that point on, whenever I looked at a potential job, I frequently asked, "When will I be done? Is this six months? Is this a year?" And then, based on that, "Is that an easy job for me? Is this challenging enough? Is this interesting enough?" Because if I think that I'm going to exit in a year, then what?

That would mean starting from scratch all over again.

Eugina Jordan calls herself a "Russian bulldozer" and laughs out loud. She is a bundle of love, inspiration, and creativity. If you ever need a pep talk on not taking no for an answer, she's your girl! She has so many amazing stories of her changing, developing, and owning her future, and many of them start with a spark. This was one of my favorites:

"I was an EA with very little impact and no growth opportunity, but one day an opportunity opened in my workplace. I created my own spark. I went to the hiring manager and offered myself for the role."

Wait! How?

"At the age of thirty-seven, newly single, with a new mortgage and a two-year-old son counting on me to provide for him, I realized that as an EA, I had little opportunity to advance. On a midwinter afternoon in 2007, I marched into my CEO's office determined to ask for his support.

"Thoughts raced through my head. I had heard about an entry-level marketing job that sounded like an opportunity for career growth. I had been considering my options carefully, and going back to school was not financially viable in my present circumstances. But this job ... this job felt like something to help me grow. I knew that, given the chance, I would succeed. All I needed was a chance to prove myself. All I needed was a yes from my boss, the CEO.

"But I am his EA. I support the whole executive team. Will he let me go?

"Anxiety roiled in the pit of my stomach as I walked into his office. I remember like it was yesterday the way the sunlight streamed through the window across his desk. His answer had the power to be life changing.

"I took a deep breath, and with no preamble, before I could change my mind, I told him, 'There is an opening in the marketing department, and I want a transfer.'

"He studied me for what felt like an eternity, then he smiled and said, 'I would miss you, but I cannot be selfish and stop your growth.'

"I didn't even realize I was holding my breath until I felt it whoosh out of me at his answer.

"And just like that, with one simple yes, I got my biggest career break."

Like I had in the past, Eugina managed to find a way to move up within her existing organization. I asked her how she'd gone about it.

"I had an excellent personal relationship with my then manager," she explains. "To this day we exchange Christmas cards, and he knew I had extra motivation, a fire in my belly to do more than what my role at the time was all about.

"I pitched myself but also focused on what was suitable for the company, not just for myself. I was known for building excellent internal relationships, being very organized, and being a quick learner. This meant the company needed to take a chance on me, but I had shown my skills in the past—transferable skills. I reminded them of those in the conversation and included my love for the company and my wish to stay and grow with it. My then boss was highly supportive. Having an internal supporter and a team that will root for your success is critical in making career advancement in the company you work for."

Reading the Signs

If you keep your eyes and ears open at work and keep yourself in a learning mindset as much as possible, spotting external sparks is almost too easy. Those kinds of sparks are everywhere—in conversations, in company announcements, in staff meetings—all hiding in plain sight. You just have to be aware of them and ready to respond to the information you uncover, if that information is relevant to you.

That, of course, is the important caveat. What counts as a spark for you might not be a spark for someone else, and vice versa. For example, in one of my previous jobs, an announcement went out that the company was bringing in a new leader who was going to be involved in diversity and inclusion. Usually when a company puts out an announcement like that—that a new executive is coming on—everyone sends congratulations and says they want to meet with the new person, but there's nothing especially urgent about it. That's how the announcement hit me—there was nothing that seemed to be related to my job, so the message was not a spark for me.

> What counts as a spark for you might not be a spark for someone else, and vice versa.

However, for a gay colleague of mine, that announcement was a big external spark. Unlike me, she had an agenda and something to contribute. She knew she belonged in those diversity conversations and had a real passion to get involved, so she wrote an email to the person in charge and essentially said, "I'm so glad there's someone with whom I can actually exchange ideas and with whom I can share my thoughts." The person in the leadership job was new and didn't even know who my colleague was, but he agreed to meet with her. And because my colleague came to him with a story about *why* she should be included in the conversation, she found herself taking forward something that she was super passionate about and having a seat at the table. She was one of the first people to consult with this new leader, a program started, she got a budget, and she filled this new role in addition to her job. Her efforts were spotlighted, her name was put forward, and because of her efforts, she was nominated for promotion.

All because she paid attention to what was basically a note.

So, how do you analyze a message for sparks—and what do those sparks mean? Remember, a new person joining the company could be an opportunity, like it was for my colleague, or it could be a threat that puts you or your job at risk. Either way, it might represent either an opportunity or a necessity to start from scratch.

When you uncover a spark, that's when you know it's time to start paying attention and getting ready for what may come next. Which, in essence, means doing the following:

- ➲ Polishing your CV and LinkedIn profile (although I recommend keeping these as up to date as possible by adding accomplishments, recommendations, and projects as they happen)

- ➲ Reactivating your PBOD (but, again, make sure you nurture it all year round)

- ➲ Opening yourself up to the outside world (I usually do talks. I try to invest in my brand, and I try to maintain a rhythm about that, but you can do anything that increases your exposure to people outside your company.)

Sometimes, if I have a new job or I'm consumed with making something happen, I slip into execution mindset and get bogged down in just doing my job. So I understand how easy it is to accidentally slip those blinders back on, even unintentionally. But it's really important to maintain your connection to the outside world. Because starting from scratch is much harder alone, and it's much easier to miss or misinterpret sparks without help. This is one area where my PBOD is really, really important. The people you know and trust can help you assess a situation, fill in any missing details, alert you to any opportunities or dangers you might not see, and just generally provide the support you need to respond to sparks and get ready to start from scratch.

> **Starting from scratch is much harder alone, and it's much easier to miss or misinterpret sparks without help.**

Ashwini Panse and I connected immediately. We were born two days apart, have kids the same age, and got married just a year apart (and found this out while laughing so hard!). But Ashwini, being the amazing ball of fire that she is, has done something we all just dream of. She used the spark generated by a major milestone to start from scratch. As Ashwini explains, "I used hitting the age of forty to restart myself from scratch. I thought that age of forty needed to be the year I did forty things I had never done before. I recommend this to anyone, really. I learned so much about myself, my family, what makes me happy, and what I'll do when I grow up. I'll never do some things again, but experiencing them was important to me. Other experiences I can't wait to do again or even do regularly."

. . . .

And If the Signs Are Real?

If your research reveals that the signs are real, there are different possible outcomes to consider:

- ➔ You may be looking at a great opportunity.

- ➔ You might get laid-off.

- ➔ You might stay where you are and be miserable.

- ➔ You might survive and thrive.

- ➔ You might move to a better position.

- ➔ You might leave for a better position.

- ➔ You might make a lateral or even downward move (especially if you panic and move too quickly).

- ➔ You might decide to do something completely different.

Spotting internal sparks and determining whether or not they're real isn't as easy, because it involves looking inward, past the surface where everything might seem fine, and listening to your own inner voice. That said, once you know what sparks to look for, it gets a lot easier to at least hear what that voice is trying to tell you. Just remember not to be afraid. Just because you're open to or even looking for those sparks doesn't necessarily mean you have to act on them. It just means you need to be aware that they're there and listen to what you're trying to tell yourself so you can make a plan for what to do next.

If you're thinking that "What's next?" might involve leaving your job and starting a new one, according to *Forbes,* there are "five undeniable signs" to look for, as follows:

1. You're unhappy most of the time you're at work.

2. Your work environment is toxic.

3. You don't enjoy or aren't comfortable doing the work.

4. You believe you're built for better (or at least different) things.

5. The outcomes you're working toward feel meaningless or negative to you.[14]

Of course, there can be other, more subtle signs that it may be time to think about scratching the itch and moving on. But there are also ways to respond to these kinds of sparks without blowing up your whole career. You have to consider the following:

→ When is it time to shut it down?

→ When is it time to turn it on?

When I took that job that wasn't right for me, I realized it within two weeks, but I still took the time to think through the right way to respond to the situation. And a big part of that was to determine what it would take for me to be done. Once I had that figured out, I created a plan to complete the work with a firm end date. I committed to accomplishing everything within that period of time. I wound up staying a year, finished everything I set out to accomplish, and was able to leave with a recommendation. Because I was really, actually *done.*

---

14   Kathy Caprino, "5 Undeniable Signs It's Time to Leave Your Job," *Forbes,* February 14, 2017, https://www.forbes.com/sites/kathycaprino/2017/02/14/5-undeniable-signs-its-time-to-leave-your-job/?sh=7c3e6e31539f.

Of course, if you're in a particularly toxic or soul-crushing situation, or if you're on the wrong end of a round of layoffs, you may not have a choice about when to respond to a spark. But even then you might have some control over your future. If you build a good name, if you build good relationships, you can open doors that will help you land on your feet and start from scratch, whether or not it happens to be your choice. And that can help ensure your next job is the best possible one for you.

Look Before You Leap

Before you jump into that next opportunity, let's have a quick talk about bad leadership.

My first bad manager had zero respect for my time outside work. When I was sick, she would call me every hour to see if I was back online (something she never did on days I wasn't sick). The second bad manager I had was always fifteen minutes late to our weekly meeting. No, I didn't care if he did it to others as well. I also had a manager who took my emails and reports and sent them on his own behalf, with no thank-yous or credit given. Today, I can identify a bad manager from a distance, and I advise my mentees to check whom they interview with. Just remember, people join companies, but they leave managers. So check before you join.

Ask questions like these:

- ➔ What do you look for in an employee?

- ➔ Why do you think I would be a fit (or not) for this role? (Did they bother getting to know you, or are they only responding to your experience?)

- ➔ What are your values? Which company value resonates with you most?

- ⊙ What will our weekly meeting look like?

- ⊙ Do you do group updates or meetings?

- ⊙ How do you build connections between team members?

- ⊙ What's fun about you? What do you do outside work?

- ⊙ How and when do you provide feedback?

These are just a few questions; you may have some of your own. And a bad manager may not be the only spark that motivates you to leave a job. Here are some personal examples:

- ⊙ I left my first job after my boss told me he saw no reason to give me a raise because I wouldn't be working any harder the next year.

- ⊙ I left my second job because I was commuting for three hours every day and felt I was reserving energy instead of giving my all so that I could drive back home.

- ⊙ I left my third job because I was introduced to a founder with an idea, and I couldn't see myself not building that product.

- ⊙ I was fired because it was 2008, and the company I worked for let 90 percent of its workforce go to try to survive. I was on maternity leave (not cool).

- ⊙ At another company, I chose not to leave during a terrible turnover because I felt that if I left at that point, there would be too much I didn't finish, and I worried I would regret it every day.

- ⊙ Although I was offered another excellent opportunity at another workplace, I didn't leave because I admired the person I was already reporting to and felt I'd grow personally and professionally if I stuck around.

What I'm getting at here is that I made choices. Who knows what would have happened if I had made others? The fact is I have zero—absolutely zero—regrets. I have gained experience that helps me in what I do today, and I met partners, friends, and mentors I am so proud to be around.

When you feel the spark, you always have a choice. You can shut it down, or you can light up the room with it. It's up to you.

Act on Your Spark

If you're feeling an internal or external spark, ask yourself these three questions about your current position:

⊖ What can I still accomplish in this job?

_____

_____

⊖ What would take regular expectations to the next level of execution?

_____

_____

⊖ What do I need to accomplish in order to be done doing the job?

_____

_____

The answers to these questions should tell you if it's time to pay attention to the spark and get ready to start from scratch.

Now that you know how to spot and analyze the sparks that let you know you're going to have to start from scratch, it's time to get down to business and actually create the new you that you need to be for this new start. Beginning in the next chapter …

CHAPTER 5:

What (or Who?) Is the New You?

Every time I start from scratch, whether it's in a new role or at a new company, I have a little ritual I go through. Once I have some idea of where or how my new start will be taking place and I've done enough research and preparation around that role to start to pursue or prepare for it, I imagine another woman standing several feet away from me. This woman possesses all the qualities I will need to thrive in my new role.

She is, in fact, my *role model.*

Let me be clear: I'm not imagining a specific person whom I know, like a mentor or a talented peer. I have those kinds of role models, too, but in this case I actually create a working *model* (in my mind, but also on paper) of the person I will need to be in order to excel in my new *role*. I'm a product manager, and designing and working with this role model is basically how I manage the project of becoming the person I need to be.

The first step in this process is gathering all the research that I've done about what it will take to start from scratch on my terms and what qualities I will need to perform this new role successfully. I'm basically talking about the product of all the steps we've covered in this book:

- I've opened myself up to more information through learning.

- I've built my resilience.

- I've started and nurtured relationships with my PBOD.

- I've done the work to determine that I'm actually *done* with my current role and know it's time to make a move.

When I reach that point, I know I'm ready for the next step, which is figuring out who I need to be to not only win the role I want but also to grow and thrive and succeed in that role.

That's what this chapter is all about.

Prabdeep Singh says, "I really think people need to invest more in knowing themselves. Really know thyself! Write down everything you know about yourself as a human and professional. Break down your skills, what you are good at, and what you lack—spend time making this list.

"Then, spend time making yourself better, both as a person and as an employee. I come from a different generation, where what you do makes you who you are, and that's how you gain respect. These days there is 'fast money' and 'crypto millionaires.' But to survive, you need to invest in having real skills. It's a journey.

"Just decide what you need to be better at, write it down, and put it in a place you can't miss. People don't always see their flaws, and I need a constant reminder, so it's here in front of me every day."

Building a Role Model

Once I know what role I'm building my model for, I do extensive research to figure out who she, just like a product I'd like to create, needs to be. It's all the research a product manager would do to build and plan a product or feature, except it's for a role, a career, an employer or job. What does the market want? What will be expected of this person? What will make her stand out as the best option against her competition?

I don't just ponder these questions for a few minutes and move on. This is a process that I put time and effort into. I take time to really think about who the ideal person for this role would be, really fleshing her out and thinking of as many aspects of her work life as I can, and then I unpack the features and qualities she will need to have to succeed in the role I want.

I do that by asking questions.

Who would I need to be to be able to fill this role? What would I need to be like? What skills would I need to have? What kind of person would I be?

These questions are the beginning of another kind of checklist—one designed specifically to help me create my role model. Because I want to get as close to that person as possible, I ask a lot of these questions, and I also write all of them down, both so I can analyze them and use them later.

My ultimate goal is to put myself in the shoes of this woman who is in this place where I want to be and imagine every possible thing I can about her life, from what she does when she gets up in the morning and what she does first to the last thing on her mind when her head hits the pillow at night. I try to unpack everything I can think of and really push myself into the corners of her work life and her long-term goals and just *who she is*. So it usually ends up taking a bit of time and winds up to be a pretty long list.

How long? Here's an idea of just some of the questions I ask. You can use them when you create your own role model at the end of this chapter, both as is and as inspiration for some questions of your own:

- ➔ What type of education certification and knowledge does this role model have?

- ➔ What does she read, and how does she learn and get updated?

- ➔ What is her work experience?

- ➔ How does she present herself in the workplace?

- ➔ Who does she need to work with daily, and what roles do they serve? What is their expertise, and how can she help them?

- ➔ How do her peers regard her and interact with her?

- ➔ How does she interact with her superiors?

- ➔ What are the expectations of her superiors from her and by hiring her?

- ➔ What is the day-to-day experience of her job?

- ➔ What is she usually busy doing?

- ➔ What tools does she need to do her job?

- ➔ Who is the first person she speaks to in the morning?

- ➔ Who is on her team and what are their skills and areas of expertise?

- ➔ Who are her peers and what are their skills and challenges?

- ➔ Who does she collaborate with?

- ➔ Who does she report to and what does that person consider an important skill for the role?

- ➔ What language do she and "her people" speak?

- ➔ What do they know?

- ➔ What do they care about?

- ➔ What tools, processes, or software does she use for her role?

- ➔ How does she grow her knowledge? (What does she read? What podcasts does she listen to? Does she volunteer or take classes?)

- ➔ Where does she have visibility at work?

- ➔ Where does she have visibility in the field?

- ➔ Does she belong to any groups or associations?

- ➔ What location does she work from?

- ➔ Does she travel for her job? How often? Where does she go?

- ➔ What does she worry about?

- ➔ What constitutes success for her?

- ➔ What will she need to do to get there?

I know that might seem like a lot, but I promise it's worth the investment. The more you know, the closer you can get to your goal. On that note, I also make sure to include a few really specific, granular questions to prepare my role model for her (my) interview, when and if the process reaches that stage. I ask the following:

- ➔ Who will probably interview this person?

- ➔ What questions will they ask?

- ➔ Which problems are they expecting to solve by hiring for that role?

In other words, I think of everything I possibly can as I envision and analyze who this new me will need to be. That's what I'm going to encourage you to do at the end of this chapter, or whenever you decide that you're ready (or need) to start from scratch.

When I've finished the list (although it takes a while to really finish, because I continue to come up with more questions to add to it once I start working with it—but that's okay!), I have a comprehensive-bordering-on-exhaustive list of the qualities my role model will have. In fact, I have an actual role model. I know what behaviors she regularly performs, what she knows, and who she *is*. That's how I can actually picture her standing several feet away from me. I know literally everything about her—because I created her!

Which means, after this process you will also know exactly who you need to be to fill the role you want when you start from scratch.

> Knowing who you should be and actually being that person are two different things.

And knowledge is power, right? Then again, knowing who you should be and actually being that person are two different things. Once you've uncovered the gaps, those places you're not at all like your role model, the next step in this process is to close those gaps so you can get closer and closer to your role model's shoes until you're actually standing in them.

That's when I turn back to the checklist.

Finding the Gaps

When I create a checklist, I don't do it only to help me design the perfect role model. I also use it to pinpoint the places where I am like my role model and, more importantly, where my role model and I are not in the same place. Realistically, I think it also helps tackle

"Imposter Syndrome" as it's a realistic list of what I know and don't. So once I reach a place where I feel like my list is close to completed, or I just get sick of asking questions and feel like answering them, I start doing that. I go down the list and answer each question with what my role model would need to have or be or do. Then I ask myself, *Do I have that? Am I ready?*

This looks different depending on whether the question is about a quality, a tool, a relationship, a skill, a piece of knowledge, or something else. However, the simplest way for me to explain how this process works is to use a simple example, like a tool. If my role model works with a tool I'm not currently using, that would be an area where there could be a gap. So I'd ask, *Do I know how to use that tool?*

Then I'd answer either yes, meaning this is an area where my role model and I are in alignment, or no, meaning there's a gap.

As I go through this process and answer each question, I notice where my role model has qualities, knowledge, or maybe even some habits or routines that I share or that are familiar to me. Those places where I write yes, where I have the right tool or relationship or skill or habit already locked down in place, I don't worry about it. The places where my role model and I are already in alignment are already a part of who I am, so I don't need to make any changes in those areas. I can check them off the list.

But there are other cases where there's a gap between me and my role model. There are things I don't know, tools I don't use, connections I don't have, qualities I haven't developed that I know my role model has, because after all, I created her. They're right there on my list!

That information right there, showing me where the gaps are between me and my role model, are like gold. Because they reveal exactly where I need to make changes and what I need to work on or adjust to if I want to give myself the best possible shot at starting from scratch in the role successfully. The gaps on my checklist are like a road map to the things I need to achieve, accomplish, become, and yes, change in order to get where I want to go. Once I know what the problems are, I can begin to solve them. Step by step, I can begin to do the things I need to do to get closer and closer to that role model until I am actually standing in her shoes.

Because, after all, they're *my* shoes.

. . . .

Carrie Collins was a senior in college, went to a career fair, and came back panicked. "I thought, 'Oh my God, I have no marketable skills.'" Off she went to law school, and later she began practicing law. She was working as a lawyer at a small firm when she realized the job wasn't for her. "I cannot keep track of my time in six-minute increments for the rest of my life," she recalls thinking.

Today, Carrie is the chief advancement and strategic planning officer of Philadelphia College of Osteopathic Medicine and the founder of H.O.W., a business consulting firm. Very far from "Carrie at the Career Fair" and even "Carrie the Clock Watcher."

How did she build the new Carrie?

"When I decided to leave the law firm, I accessed every tool I had. I get things done, and I show results—no matter what I'm doing. As a lawyer, the work is very transactional, as that's how you're measured, but in my life, I was both a planner and super efficient, and I realized I could use all those skills at a new job. I'm a quick study, so I wasn't afraid to go after a job that I had only a partial background in, and the rest I researched and trusted my ideas and instincts. Gotta love Google!

"Looking back, I had the opposite of imposter syndrome. I embraced the 'fake it 'til you make it' approach, knowing exactly what I can do and haven't yet learned to do, and I worked a lot behind the scenes to figure things out.

"Today, I know my superpower is taking a lot of information, synthesizing it, and building a new story."

. . . .

Closing the Gaps

What I really love about this process is that when I close the gaps between me and my role model, it's like going back to school—except that I designed the course myself because I know exactly where it is that I need to get to. Basically, it's reverse engineering. You want to reach something, to achieve a specific goal, and in order to get there and understand how it works, you need to first look at the end result you're trying to achieve. It's like reading the code of something that was already done and realizing, *Oh, so that's how you do it.*

Years ago I met the founder of Ringly, a company that built an IOT device that looks like a bracelet. That was her goal—to make something like an Apple Watch, a device that's connected to your phone and sends you notifications, but instead of a sporty watch, it looks like a piece of fine jewelry that you could wear with a cocktail dress. And in her vision, she didn't just want the device itself to reflect this aesthetic. She wanted everything, right down to the charger, to be about luxury and bling and send a consistent message that this product was a piece of jewelry. In her mind, that meant the bracelet absolutely could not have a regular plastic charger. You don't stick a hunk of plastic into a piece of fine jewelry! She told her engineers that she wanted the charger to look like a jewelry box, so when the wearer took the bracelet off to charge it, the experience would be similar to the experience of putting a special piece of jewelry away for safekeeping.

Interestingly, no one on her engineering team had the faintest idea how to build a jewelry box, let alone a charger that looked like a jewelry box. So, in order to fulfill their vision and create this product, they had to reverse engineer it. How could they fit the function to the form? They took other charging devices and dismantled them and looked at the components they would need to have in theirs. Then they said, "Okay. These are the components we need. Now we just need to figure out how to get them all into a jewelry box and make it work." It would look different, but the function would be the same.

That's reverse engineering—looking at the end result, going backward until you understand how to build something, and then building it according to what you've learned.

So let's look at your role model as your end result—she is who you need to be to start from scratch in the particular role you designed her to fill. When you reverse engineer the new you, you look at what you need to add to the current you to make her more like that role model and inch her closer to those shoes.

Once I identify the gaps between me and my role model, I ask, "What will it take in order for me to behave this way, talk this way, act this way, know these things?" Each question that reveals a gap essentially reveals a problem that needs solving, so I try to answer each of those questions by writing down what or who would be able to help me close those gaps. By *what* I mean resources, and by *who* I mean people. Then I just start googling and finding blogs and podcasts and books that will help me turn those nos into yeses and start getting more in alignment with my role model. Once I have done all that, I basically have my learning list to grow into the new me.

And after that, it's easy. I make time to sit down and read, or listen to podcasts, or take a class and learn, or interact with people, or ask my PBOD for advice and suggestions, or whatever else I need to do in order to close the gaps. Usually a combination of all these things and more.

Sometimes getting closer to your role model's shoes also involves developing new habits. There may be routines that help her stay on top of the things she needs to know and/or accomplish in her life that are not part of your experience. But how do you develop a new habit? The *New York Times* suggests piggybacking your new habit onto a habit you already have, like listening to podcasts instead of music when you work out or reading the kinds of materials your role model would read along with your morning coffee.[15] Many people follow the "21/90 rule," which claims that it takes twenty-one days to form a habit and three months to turn that habit into a lifestyle change. Personally, I'm a believer in doing whatever works best for you.

The point is, if you want something, there are things you can do to help make it happen. You aren't powerless. You don't need to be lucky. You just need to have a plan. If someone says to me, "I want to have your role someday," my first question is always, "What are you doing in order to do that?" Because if you want to grow into any role, you need to be doing something to encourage that growth. So I ask, "Do you volunteer in other organizations? What do

> **You aren't powerless. You don't need to be lucky. You just need to have a plan.**

---

15   Tara Parker-Pope, "How to Build Healthy Habits," *New York Times*, February 18, 2020, https://www.nytimes.com/2020/02/18/well/mind/how-to-build-healthy-habits. html?.?mc=aud_dev&ad-keywords=auddevgate&gclid=Cj0KCQjw7MGJBhD-ARIsAMZ0eeuNcaQs_BSyLNDcvv9mRa7-_2CIIOyUvzvkQeoCK7JU2MAyYYdfVj8aA pakEALw_wcB&gclsrc=aw.ds.

you read? How do you learn? How do you grow? How are you moving in that direction?" If you expect to come to my organization, sit there for a few years, and one day magically wind up in my job, well … that's just not going to happen. You have to actively be working, pretty much all the time, to become the person you need to be. After all, life doesn't stand still. And that means another opportunity to start from scratch is always around the corner. It's always good to be ready.

But What If the Gaps Still Don't Close?

So you're probably wondering, *If I follow all the steps I've laid out so far, and I'm really, really committed, do I always end up exactly where I want to be, standing firmly in my role model's shoes, knowing I'm 100 percent ready to charge into my new role and this next chapter of my life and kick its ass?*

Of course not.

This is still real life, and in real life you don't always get what you want, or even what you deserve. But I promise you, no matter what, whatever work you have done toward building this role model will put you ahead of the game. However, if you've put whatever you've been able to put into closing the gap between you and your role model, and there's some kind of time crunch where you have to move from the preparing phase to the actually doing it phase and your role model's shoes are still at least a foot or two away, there are a few things you can do.

First, ask yourself these questions:

⊛ What does success look like when you see it as this different version of yourself?

⊛ What would your team need from you for this success to happen?

➲ Do you have the skills to succeed in the role?

➲ Do you need to learn something new that someone needs to help you with, or can you actually learn it alone?

➲ What are your chances of succeeding right now? Do you need to do some legwork?

➲ Do you have partners within the organization who will help you build your story so that it makes sense? The more people who say that X is needed, the more credibility you'll have when you say that you can do X.

Once you've answered those questions, based on those answers you have a few options for moving forward:

1. If you feel like you've closed enough of the gaps to perform the role if you get it, you can go ahead and go for it anyway. You may be at some disadvantage, but you will also know you've done a lot of work to get where you are, and thanks to the checklist you've created, you have (and can articulate) a clear plan to keep working on what you need to work on—meaning you will get closer and closer to your role model's shoes even as you try to win, or even perform, her role.

2. You can adjust your goal to some sort of compromise point and readjust your role model to fit those new, likely less stringent parameters. There's no reason you can't make a strong start from scratch in a different role than the one you initially wanted or envisioned for yourself. You can continue to work on the gaps in your checklist so you will eventually get where you want to go. Or you may decide you want to go somewhere else entirely, because you've learned and grown in a different direction.

3. You may find an opportunity to start from scratch within your current organization and decide, *Oh, I can park here, and maybe this could be a good thing for the next two or three years*. And then, of course, continue to build your relationships and continue to work on that checklist, or readjust, or even create a whole new role model if your goals change.

4. If the worst thing happens and you can't pursue that spark no matter how much you want to and how much you've prepared to move into a new role, you can still find opportunities in your current one. When there's no place to jump to, you can still use the relationships you have built inside the organization to grow into the role you want while you continue to do your job. And while you're there, you'll continue to grow your qualifications and credentials, and the next thing you know, the gaps between you and your role model won't be as big.

The thing to remember is, it's all a journey. You're working and preparing to start from scratch on your own terms, but you're not necessarily going to be starting from scratch for the very last time, because your next role is probably not your final destination. There will be a lot of stops on the way, and each time you stop, you need to get ready for it all over again and assess how far it will get you in terms of where you're trying to get overall, and wait for a spark, and determine when you're done, and read the signs, and finally start from scratch again. Maybe you won't have to survive as many reorgs as I did. But if life never changed, we'd never learn anything or grow, and at least to me, that sounds boring. We might as well embrace it and enjoy the ride and squeeze everything out of it that we possibly can.

Some Questions to Get You Thinking ...

You know how people have certain interview questions in their bank that they like to pull out during an interview? My personal favorite is "What do you want to be when you grow up?" Because I feel like that question unpacks so much. It shows me somebody's passion and vision and direction and focus. I don't necessarily zero in on exactly what they're saying; it's more about how passionate they are, how driven they are.

But there's one other thing I also consider.

Do they have a plan?

In my line of work, I know if you don't have a plan for your life, then you're probably not going to have a very good plan for my product! So to close out this chapter, I'm going to help you jump start your own plan for the new you by designing your product, i.e. your life, the right way.

Build Your Own Checklist

Now that you've seen how I create my role model and how I use her to prepare to start from scratch, it's time for you to create your own.

1. Start by imagining a new role—either one that you know you will be starting from scratch in, or even better, one that you really, really want. Or if you need to start from scratch in your personal life, imagine starting from scratch in whatever new situation you're facing or thinking about facing.

    Describe it here:

    > *Tip:* You can use an introduction format. "Meet Jane. She is... She comes from... She is a specialist in..."

    _____

    _____

    _____

    _____

    _____

2. Create a list of questions to help you understand who your role model is. Remember, your goal is to unpack everything you can about this person so you can eventually figure out what it will take for you to stand in her shoes. You can go back to the questions I wrote down earlier in the chapter for inspiration—there are a lot of them! And, since you know more about the role you're creating a model for than I do, you'll likely have some questions of your own.

_____

_____

_____

_____

_____

3. Imagine the person who would succeed in that new role. This will be your role model. Remember, this does not need to be a real person, but a person of your imagination. Unpack their behavior, skills, knowledge, and habits.

Write their characteristics here:

> *Tip:* Write all characteristics. Don't focus on whether you have those or not, we will handle those in the next exercise.

CHARACTERISTIC	DO I HAVE IT?

4. Go back through your list, and answer all the questions. Then ask if you have whatever the question specifies, and write *yes* or *no*.

5. Look at the places where you wrote *no*. Those are the gaps between you and your role model.

For each place you wrote *no,* come up with a solution that will help you transform it into a *yes.* This list is important to keep and work on with your personal board of directors. If you don't know how to close the gap, maybe they have good advice.

CAPABILITY/ CHARACTERISTICS I DON'T OWN	
HOW DO I CLOSE THE GAP?	

CAPABILITY/ CHARACTERISTICS I DON'T OWN	
HOW DO I CLOSE THE GAP?	

CAPABILITY/ CHARACTERISTICS I DON'T OWN	
HOW DO I CLOSE THE GAP?	

CAPABILITY/ CHARACTERISTICS I DON'T OWN	
HOW DO I CLOSE THE GAP?	

CAPABILITY/ CHARACTERISTICS I DON'T OWN	
HOW DO I CLOSE THE GAP?	

Congratulations. You've built your vision. In the next chapter, we will put that vision together and bring her to life.

CHAPTER 6:

Bringing Your Vision to Life

When I was at AOL, I got obsessed with the idea of building an incubator or an innovation program for new concepts. Our then CTO kept holding hackathons, where the tech organization (product, engineering, design, and more) would all get together for twenty-four or forty-eight hours to brainstorm new innovations and build proofs of concept. I would always enter, and I always did well. My team would win first, second, or third place, and everyone would congratulate me. But in the end, it in fact meant nothing other than that recognition. We never implemented any of the ideas. Not mine, and not anyone else's. We never did anything with them at all.

Eventually, I decided not to participate at the next hackathon. On hackathon day, while all the participants came to work in their hackathon-themed shirts, I walked around dressed in my normal clothes, quite happy with my decision to not stress out, participate, and hence not wear that shirt. Sure enough, the CTO, who was walking on our floor looking for the participants in their shirts, spotted me. He looked at me with surprise and asked me why I wasn't wearing the shirt. Then he asked, "Are you really not participating?" He seemed disappointed, which made sense, because I was a recognized participant. Finally, he asked me the question I was waiting for: Why wasn't I participating? I had my answer prepared: "Because I'll win it," I said, "and you won't do anything with it."

Surprisingly, the CTO was not at all shocked by my answer. It turned out he had been talking with the CEO about the very same issue, i.e. that employees pitch great ideas or new product directions but are so heads-down or resource-constrained that they are unable to bring those to launch. That was when I decided I wanted to be the person to create our company's new innovation center, or incubator for bringing new ideas to launch. I wanted that to be my role. And since this was a role that had never existed before in the company, as well as something I had never done before, I had to start everything from scratch. Assuming I'd get it, I had to build the role itself and then build myself into the person who would fill it. Which might sound like a little bit of a cheat or head start, but since I had never done anything like this before, I had a lot of work to do. I had never been part of an incubator/accelerator or innovation program before. Early in my career, when I started in consulting, I was often visiting accelerators and tried to pitch my services to early-stage companies, but other than that, I really didn't have much information, especially when it came to what it meant to run one.

It was going to take a lot of work to create this role model, let alone bring her to life.

The first thing I did was, of course, google. I looked up "successful incubators" and "why incubators fail" so I could get an idea of what to do and what not to do. I read about various programs and incubators, startup hubs, innovation programs (as they all have similar characteristics and offerings) and started looking at specific blogs and content sites that were relevant to that industry. This gave me a general idea of the pieces I would need in order to build an incubator at AOL and what it might include.

Next, I went back to my research on successes and failures and googled (and LinkedIn-ed) the people involved. I tracked down the leaders of the programs I'd read about and reached out to them cold via email or LinkedIn, keeping in mind that they were busy and trying to make sure a conversation offered something for them. We had a barista on site (workplace perk) and the AOL/Verizon brand, so some people answered my invitation to meet over coffee while others did not. However, one of the people who did answer invited me to an event where other heads of accelerators would be—which was an incredibly lucky break.

I went to the event and asked each of the people I talked to to really unpack their job for me. I quickly learned that while all accelerators have the same pillars—there's an investment, there's programming or content, and there's a selection process—they all did it differently. Some said, "Hundreds of companies come to us, and we choose ten." Others said, "We get ten applicants, and we choose ten because our filtering process is so stringent from the beginning." I began to understand the differences between filters, which helped me determine what kind of application filter I would build.

I also asked each person what kind of experience the head of such program would need so I could identify which qualities and skills I had and which I would need to work on. I asked if there were other areas of expertise that that role would benefit from. How would an ex-engineer, a product manager, a designer, or a marketer approach the role? What other things might the role include? I asked what career paths these people had followed before that role and where they saw themselves going next so I would be able to understand how a move like this would fit into my own path. Would this be a pivot that would

… pardon my French … f*** up my CV? Or would it actually be seen as progress and something natural?

I asked each person about their stakeholders. Who else were they working with? What were their roles? I learned that in the world of incubators/accelerators, there would be a lot of interaction with finance and HR. These were both areas in which I did not have a lot of expertise, so I knew I would need to up my game in those areas. I interviewed more people based on those learnings and centered my questions around what working with people in those roles would entail.

Before I entered this new world, I had assumed the heads of incubators/accelerators competed with each other. My conversations with insiders showed me that there's actually a lot of collaboration in the community and that heading an incubator/accelerator is a very collaborative role. So, after that first event, I continued to attend whatever accelerator-based get-togethers or meetups were available. I needed to become part of a community where I would continue to grow and learn from their experience and get support once I actually started working in the role. As an introvert, this wasn't my favorite part of the process, but I understood that it came with the territory. If I planned to step into this role and do it effectively, I would need to go to events and do speaking engagements and actively participate in this community.

As I continued to educate myself, I learned that for innovation programs to succeed, there were aspects of HR, finance, and legal relationships that I would need to sort out. This would all be new to me—I worked with HR when I hired people or let someone go, but in this role, they would be my partners in a very different way. I also had to educate myself about the investment side. I listened to podcasts and bought books on the subjects, which I read to understand the jargon and the ecosystem and to fill in the holes of knowledge I didn't have.

After I had done all that, I started building my plan for the role itself.

I presented my plan for the role internally first, to people who knew the company, knew me, knew the organization, and understood the problem I was trying to solve. They gave me feedback, shared some concerns, and alerted me to some things that I hadn't covered—and some that I hadn't even thought of. Then I took what I learned from them, went back to the drawing board, and worked on closing the gaps. Finally, when I was satisfied that I had an airtight plan, I went outside the circle of my organization and presented it to my internal board of directors.

By this point, my plan looked spotless. I had covered all the bases. I'd done good research. I'd planned for things that might not go well and involved the right people in the process. I won the role I created and was able to start the incubator and make sure it delivered on its promise. And it did. We had hundreds of ideas generated and established a new way for the company to look at innovation—not to mention an engine that attracted new talent. Suddenly, we actually had a new story to tell of amazing innovations and access to technology and access to the resources you needed to actually get stuff done.

I had not only created my role model and her role, I was able to excel in the role—because I did the necessary preparation.

Getting Ready

When you finally land, or get close to landing, the role you've been aiming for and it's time to step into your role model's shoes, like me, you're going to discover that those shoes probably aren't going to fit … at least not perfectly.

The good news is, that's exactly how you want it.

If I already know everything I need to know to do a job well, to me that's boring. I want every new role to teach me something, to grow my skills and my knowledge and my impact in my field, because

I want to keep getting better, and I want my career path to keep pushing me forward. So for me, the right role is something that makes me better than the role model I created, no matter how much work I put into building her in the first place. It takes me places I didn't expect to go and teaches me things that weren't even on my radar.

Otherwise, what's the point (besides earning a living, obviously)?

Part of the fun of starting from scratch—and yes, there is fun involved—is the chance to push yourself beyond your limits and uncover superpowers you didn't know you had. That doesn't happen when you stay in the same place, doing the same thing you're comfortable doing month after month. And it can't happen in a new role if you already know it backward and forward. So get comfortable with the idea of not being 100 percent comfortable. That's exactly where you want to be when you start from scratch.

May Piamenta explains, "When I first started Vee, many people were focusing on my age and the fact I was a CEO at twenty-two. That's natural, and I'd probably react this way, too, but once I embraced it, it stopped taking over the room, and people started seeing that I didn't see it as a limitation but as an advantage. At the age of twenty-two, I have nothing but to make this company a success and give my all to it. As a strength, people buy into it, buy into my mission to make it a success, and are happy to join me. With that said, I am investing in them to make them, not just me, better, and Vee will grow alongside and thanks to their personal growth."

Starting a company at twenty-two initially led May to hire people who were "older and wiser," but her thinking has evolved. "When we were getting started, we hired people who knew everything, had vast experience, and it ended up being wrong for Vee. From my experience, at least when one gets started, it's best to hire people who know 70 percent of their role. This potential gap allows them to flex, learn, adjust well, and grow with the company."

I'll outline the specific steps I went through to start making up some of my own missing percentage points, so you'll be ready to not only fill your role model's shoes but eventually outgrow them.

Tailoring the Model to the Role

When you designed your role model, you built that person with a general idea of who they needed to be to fill the kind of role you were looking for. Once you have a specific role in mind, you can compare that role to the list you created when you built your role model in the last chapter to see where they do and don't align.

If there's a job description attached to your role (unlike the one I just told you about), that's an excellent place to start. When you read it thoroughly, you'll see a list of qualities the person who fills your role should have, things they should be able to do, things they should know, and the kind of experience they should have. Chances are you're not going to be able to tick all those boxes right now, and that's okay. Remember, you don't want to be at 100 percent, or you're not going to grow and you're going to get bored quickly. The goal here is to get as close as possible while specifically tailoring these final tweaks of your role model to the actual role.

If you have a job description, read everything written in the job description, or if there isn't a written job description (for example when you start from scratch by being promoted or reinventing your role), compile a list of everything you know about the job. Then, take some time to thoroughly unpack it. Where are the differences between the role you will be filling and the role model you built? You don't have to do this alone. Talk to more people like someone in this role at a different company or peers that this role will work with and unpack the needed skills. Zero in on those areas that didn't come up, that you didn't focus on, or that you didn't fully develop. You may end up with a fairly short list of places where there's a gap between your role model and the role, or you may wind up, like I did, with a really, really long one. Don't worry if your list is long—ticking off those missing boxes is where the growth that comes with your new role is going to happen.

There are two basic ways to acquire the new knowledge and skills you need to bring your role model to life. You can learn some things on your own by reading, taking courses, listening to podcasts, working as a volunteer, etc. Then there are things you can only really learn by sitting down and talking with other people and letting them immerse you in their world.

Let's look at the things you can do on your own first, before moving into the interpersonal part.

The Learning Part

Gaining the skills, language, and work style necessary to fill a new role can be daunting. You can't possibly listen to every podcast and read every book and article and LinkedIn post (although you can certainly try!). What you can do, and what you will need to do more than once in this phase, is prioritize. Focus on the key things you need to know to build the strongest possible foundation to work from. That includes not only what you need to know to do your job but also things that will make you a more well-rounded person in the role—things like the ecosystem, the language, the market, who your customers are, etc. The goal is to get a more holistic view of your role and the unique way that only you can fill it.

The next step in this process is to integrate the things you learn into your life so they become second nature. There's a difference between learning something and *knowing* it —how many times have you read an article or listened to a podcast and within a few days completely forgotten what you learned? The challenge is to take whatever you've read or listened to or done to the next level so the knowledge sticks with you and becomes a part of you. What will it take to get you to that level of comfort? Is it to read more around that topic? Or is it to summarize what you've learned as a blog post or an article on LinkedIn?

> There's a difference between learning something and knowing it.

Back in the first chapter, we spent some time talking about learning styles. If you don't remember right now, check back to see what your own learning styles are. What helps you retain information? Taking that extra step of putting what you learned into practice will help make that thing a part of you. Because you don't want to simply have tried it, attempted it, done it, and moved on. You're building a new you, so ultimately you want whatever you learn to be integrated into the person that you become.

Mariana Kobayashi felt the spark that change was coming when she realized consulting work, where she was concentrating her energy, was not for her. She decided to spend a year becoming the person she wanted to be. And because, as she told me, "I'm a planner," she came up with a list of at least thirty things she needed to know or do to land a job that would encompass who she was planning to become.

Then, she spent a year documenting her journey.

January 2021:
Moved from Berlin to Lisbon, and COVID-19 got me stuck at home. Heartbreak. No career direction. My anxiety was the worst it has ever been. Gave up my smartphone.

February 2021:
Ended my gap year. Started applying for jobs. Got serious about writing my book. Felt impostor syndrome and rejection. Too many anxiety attacks. Started Surf the Job. Got a C1 certificate in Spanish.

March 2021:
Moved to Guinea-Bissau for an internship at the bank. Got back my smartphone. Regained my heritage. Job shadowed four people.

April 2021:
Started creating content on LinkedIn. Had five coffee talks a week. Got some career direction.

May 2021:
Moved into a room in Lisbon with friends. Started an internship at Accenture.

June 2021:
After I'd been connected with Jonathan for some time, he invited me to join Wonsulting. Started making the most of remote working (traveling). Started the Gen Z Whys podcast.

July 2021:
Attempted to break a Guinness World Record (#kobayashirunningchallenge) and created the first network for mental health in Portugal. Rejected a full-time offer.

August 2021:

Got the open water certificate. Started learning web dev at Le Wagon. Joined the building team of Ready2Start. Did 250+ free LinkedIn reviews. Interviewed for my dream company.

September 2021:

Obtained my web dev certificate and continued learning about tech. My mental health started sinking again managing my nine-to-five, side projects, and personal issues. Released an ebook, Productivity Might Be Killing You. Started going to acupuncture.

October 2021:

Joined Startup Jobs Portugal. Ended Surf the Job. Got an offer for an internship position at BCG Digital Ventures in Berlin. Released the book Eating Disorders, Love and Existential Crisis. Broke five thousand followers on LinkedIn.

November 2021:

Started a new podcast—Coffee Talk—and interviewed Jerry Lee. Was invited to three public speaking events and two podcasts. A friend died. Burned out. Finished my job at Ready2Start. Booked a ticket to India.

December 2021:

Went offline. Found a new balance. Read fourteen-plus books. Did a hundred hours of yoga. Met incredible people. Started doing freelance jobs. Moved to Berlin. Redefined priorities.

The moral of the story? You can change your life in one year!

The People Part

Reading articles and listening to podcasts can only get you so far. In order to fully understand a role and what it involves, you're going to need to talk with actual humans. Which is also a challenge. Most people are busy with their own lives and careers and may not be excited about giving their time to just anyone for any reason. That's why, when you reach out to people for help, especially if you don't know them personally, you need to approach them the right way. If your goal is to get people to help you, you need to start by treating them with respect.

> **If your goal is to get people to help you, you need to start by treating them with respect.**

That means, when you zero in on a role and source you need to meet with, take time to learn something about a person before you cold contact them. Check their LinkedIn profile, google them, ask people who know them about them (in a low-key, not-stalker-y way). Your goal is to find some way to connect with them on a human-to-human level, something to make the conversation less awkward and more productive, so try to learn something that makes them interesting, or something they struggle with, or what interests them. In other words, find a way to reach out without making it all about you. Because, not to be mean, but who cares about you? If you think they are worth contacting, many others probably do, too. You want to stick out in the crowd.

I'm telling you this because I get approached by people looking for help and/or advice all the time. And when I get a LinkedIn message from someone saying something like "So I saw this job; could you meet with me for five minutes and tell me more about it?" guess how it makes me feel? It certainly doesn't make me want to take time out of my busy schedule to help this person.

I can't tell you how many messages I've gotten consisting of some version of "Hey, can you give me some tips on how to find a job where you work?"

Here are just a few examples from my LinkedIn feed of things people actually expect me to do for them. I promise, these are all 100 percent real.

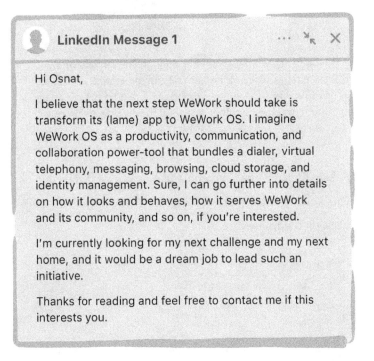

LinkedIn Message 1

Hi Osnat,

I believe that the next step WeWork should take is transform its (lame) app to WeWork OS. I imagine WeWork OS as a productivity, communication, and collaboration power-tool that bundles a dialer, virtual telephony, messaging, browsing, cloud storage, and identity management. Sure, I can go further into details on how it looks and behaves, how it serves WeWork and its community, and so on, if you're interested.

I'm currently looking for my next challenge and my next home, and it would be a dream job to lead such an initiative.

Thanks for reading and feel free to contact me if this interests you.

In this note, the writer starts his message by insulting my peers. Perhaps this person tried to sound knowledgeable, but they actually made several wrong assumptions about the business direction, and they presented an aggressive and short-sighted approach.

Instead of assuming why you can do better job than those already doing it, talk about your experience and explain how spending a brief time with you would benefit or interest me.

LinkedIn Message 2   ··· ⌐ ✕

Hi Osnat,

I hope this msg reaches you well.

Please consider recommending me for this role, details below.

Thank you, and hope to meet one day soon.

Jane Doe

I came across the PxWe Experience Design Manager, US East at WeWork and am interested in applying. Would you be open to sharing my LinkedIn profile with the hiring team so they know about my interest in this role?

Asking for someone's recommendation is a lot if they don't know you. You can share more about yourself and help them make that decision themsleves.

LinkedIn Message 3   ··· ⌐ ✕

Hi Osnat,

Hope all is well with you! I came across the Account Manager at WeWork and am interested in applying. Would you be open to sharing my LinkedIn profile with the hiring team so they know about my interest in this role?

Here's a link to the job I'm interested in:

https:...

This is a template offered by LinkedIn. I have received this exact message hundreds of times in my inbox. If you want a stranger's support, make your message personal to them and you.

LinkedIn Message 4 ⤢ ✕

Hi Osnat!

I can imagine you being very busy—so I appreciate you connecting with me! Hope you're doing well. Would you be open to chat for 15 minutes or so this week?

I'm available all day on Friday. If not, I'm also free in the morning on Monday. Happy to also provide times for later in the week if it's better, or after that. Of course, I'm open to working around any availability you have—just trying to make it easy to select times!

Warmest regards,

John Doe

> This offer feels very pushy. If the writer really appreciates my time, they should briefly explain what they want to talk about first and confirm my interest.

On the other hand, if you want to talk to me about my role, or you heard that I am involved in a specific initiative, or you saw something I posted on LinkedIn and you want to see how you can help, or you had an idea that might interest me, then I'm all ears. Just think about what's in it for the person on the other side as opposed to expecting them to patiently answer your questions. What's in it for them? Why should they take the time to talk to you? If you want to meet with someone to get information about a role or a company, be intentional about it. Do your homework so you save time for the person, and don't waste it asking questions you could have answered with an online search. Approach them in a way that generates their interest, that offers them something, so they'll think, *That person actually bothered.* Like the woman who contacted me because she listened to my podcast and wanted to debate me. That generated my interest. That got me to say yes.

Following and connecting with individuals who paved a similar path to the one you are about to be on is always a great way to start. Those people are usually busy and probably harder to access. Follow them on social media, and see if they have an upcoming speaking engagement—maybe your questions can be answered in the Q&A section of that talk. You can also always read their posts and comment with your question. It's a respectful way in!

Meeting Prep

Landing a meeting is great, but it's only a first step. The meeting itself is where you'll really have an opportunity to shine—or, if you're not careful, crash and burn. Your purpose may be to gain information; however, the person you talk to is of course going to form an impression of you—meaning a meeting is another opportunity to build your brand. So show up armed with knowledge. Be able to demonstrate some understanding not only of the role but of the company and, most importantly, some interest in the person you're meeting.

When you're researching a company, every medium has something to offer. Look for blogs, podcasts, articles, even TV segments about the company or industry or appearances by notable figures. Follow the company on LinkedIn; at least read the company posts or do a simple search and see what turns up about them. You want to look for both good things and bad things—the goal is to have as complete a picture of the environment as you can get. Learn about the company, the culture, the ecosystem, what they care about, the things they promote. Look at the management team, and learn what you can about them. In addition to anything you can get from a Google search, look at their LinkedIn posts.

If you're researching a tech company, more likely than not, you can do a lot of this work on one site called BuiltIn. BuiltIn posts content sponsored by tech companies, including companies that are hiring. The articles might seem fluffy and unsubstantial—they tend to include a lot of what the company wants to message out, like content about office culture or about how they redesigned their building, or articles with titles like "Ten Companies That Hire More Than 50 Percent Women." However, behind all that happy talk is a lot of insight into company culture as well as the kind of basic information about the company and the people and the general environment that can help you get a really clear picture. Some articles also highlight individuals and their accomplishments—and a person who has just appeared in a BuiltIn article would probably expect people (like you?) to reach out to them.

Once you've done your research on the company and the person you will be talking to, turn your focus to the role itself. Are other people currently working in that same role? If there are, learn who they are, what they know, what their background is, where they went to school, what their previous roles were, etc. And, of course, try to set up a meeting. Anyone performing the same role you're looking at is a person worth talking to. Plus, chances are they'll want to talk to you. Since you might be their colleague, they'll have a vested interest in getting to know you, if only to weigh in with their own opinion.

Meeting Dos and Don'ts

During a meeting, whether it's in person or online, it's important to remember that the person you're meeting with gave you their time— whether it's five minutes or an hour. So you want to do everything you can to make things easy for them. Come with real questions, meaning not the kind of questions you can google. That's just embarrassing, and it's the opposite of respecting a person and their time. A good rule is to come with two or three strong questions that will spark the kind of conversation you want to have and give you information that will be useful to you down the line. Have your must-ask questions ready to tackle first, and leave the less crucial questions for later. And don't expect to get a full hour of this person's time, or even all the time you want or need to get all your questions answered. If the person tells you they're ready to wrap things up and you still have more questions, thank them for their time, and mention you still have a few more questions that you'd like to ask (which can sound like a positive if you frame it right and come off as really interested and not stalker-y), and ask if it's okay to email or even meet again to follow up.

If the person felt that meeting you was valuable for them, they might agree to a second meeting or even continue the conversation right there. (If that happens, remember they are giving you extra time, and be extra conscious of the fact that they're going out of their way.) If another meeting is not on the agenda, an email can also continue the conversation. Just be sure to start with a big thank-you for the meeting you already had, summarizing what you learned and what you found most helpful. That helps build the relationship between you and the person and gives some closure to the conversation. It also shows them you invested in listening and learning and their time was extremely well spent. You will be surprised how many people agree to give free support and advice because the feeling of simply paying it forward or doing good.

Keeping Relationships Strong

Maya Angelou famously said, "People will forget what you said, people will forget what you did, but people will never forget how you made them feel." Part of bringing your role model to life is fleshing them out with the kind of actions that make people want to continue their relationships with you. When someone helps you, go back to that person and let them know, "Hey, you helped me, and I did it," or "You helped me, and I learned (fill in the blank)," or even "You helped me, but I'm still looking." It's more than good manners; it's an opportunity to remind that person that you are thankful, you exist, and are interested in them and what they do.

It makes people feel good when you acknowledge their help. Conversely, and maybe more importantly, it can make them feel bad when you don't. For example, a woman contacted me looking for a job in marketing at my company and requested to meet to learn more and to better prepare for her upcoming interview. I looked at her CV and thought it was interesting, and since I worked with that team closely, I actually thought she could be a great fit and potentially an excellent future colleague. So I agreed to meet with her, and initially everything was great. She came to our meeting prepared with questions about the company and our people, although she already knew a lot about both, because it was clear she had done her research. She asked me what projects we were working on and told me about her own projects and ideas that she thought would be interesting. I was impressed.

At the end of our conversation, she asked if I would be able to put in a good word for her at the company. Even though I was impressed, I had just met her, so I said, "I can tell them you were very diligent in your research and very pleasant and that I found several things you said very relevant, but I'm also going to tell them that you reached out to me—I'm not going to tell them you're my best friend and I know a lot about you." She said that was great and thanked me, and since I really did think she was a good fit, I recommended her. And then I totally forgot about it.

A few months later, I was at the workplace coffee area, and this person said, "Oh, hi." I looked at her and thought, *Who is she?* I knew

I'd met her before, I knew I knew her in some way, but I couldn't put my finger on it. Then she said, "I got the job!" And I realized, *Oh my God, it's her.* She had changed her hair or something, so I didn't recognize her.

And then I actually got a little angry.

Really? I thought. *This is how I find out?* Of course, I didn't say that, but I did ask, "Did you just join?" She said, "No, I actually joined like a month ago." *Really?* I thought that was a little rude. Frankly, I don't really know if my recommendation helped her, but it's still nice to acknowledge a person who took time out of their day to talk to you. Especially since, once she took the job, we were going to be coworkers. Why leave someone with the impression that you don't care, or any kind of bad feeling, when you don't have to?

The moral of my story is, don't be like that person. Send an email or a message saying, "Hey, I got the job. Thanks for taking the time and talking to me." Be a human. People will remember.

Reaching Out Effectively

I once got an email from a woman who reached out to me, not for a job but for help. Whatever role model she created, she definitely wasn't a very effective one, because this woman had sent out like two hundred CVs and had been on around a hundred interviews, and nothing was working. She wrote to me saying, "In your career, you probably interviewed many people like me. And I would like to know this: What am I missing?"

It was such an unusual and honest request, and she seemed sincere, so I really wanted to help her. I set up a meeting, and when I spoke to her, I said, "Do you mind if I interview you? Let's just do a mock interview."

So we did. I started asking the same questions an interviewer would ask, and almost immediately I learned her experience was in another area. Maybe that was the problem those hundred potential employers were having? I asked her why she was pursuing the types of roles she had been pursuing, and when she explained her reasoning, her explanation wasn't very crisp. I knew it wasn't enough to help those two hundred potential employers get past the barrier of her lack of experience. So I told her to explain her reasoning again, and the second time, it was much clearer. I explained how she could position herself in her introduction letter to get that information out of the way and counter it immediately by saying, "I know I'm not experienced in this and this, but I do have experience in this, this, and this, and that's why I'm a fit. And I would love to have a meeting with you. And here's my CV."

As our conversation continued, the woman revealed that even though she was still looking, she had actually taken another job and had been working there for about two months. I asked why she'd taken a job that wasn't right for her, and she told me, "I thought that it was a good opportunity, and it was a good company. I didn't want the job, but I wanted the company. So I thought it would be a way in."

I'd done the same thing earlier in my career, when I took a job based on the person I would be working for and ended up realizing I had made a mistake. But I didn't start looking for another job when that happened. I knew that even though the role was not a fit for me, quitting and moving on to another job before accomplishing what I had been hired to accomplish wouldn't be good for my career. I explained all this to the woman I was interviewing. I told her she could actually ruin her relationships at a company she wanted to work for so badly by coming in with an attitude of *Let me just get a foot in the door,* only to move on to the next thing the minute a better opportunity came along. I told her that wasn't honest, and it would be a stain on her CV—a dishonest thing she would need to explain to everyone who interviewed her in her career going forward, at least for a while. I advised her to try to stick it out and find a role in the same place in her same discipline and try to grow from there.

The woman was actually pretty distraught after looking for a job for so long and finding nothing that met her needs. Our meeting ran long because I didn't want to cut her short. But after she left, I didn't hear from her for two days. I started to wonder if our conversation had been yet another waste of my time. Then she emailed me. The email was really candid—she told me she took everything I said to her seriously and that she had come to understand some things about herself. Then she wrote a list of the things she had learned, some of which were pretty harsh. I felt like the assessment was going to help her in the long run, but I couldn't help wondering if she'd been so hard on herself because of anything I said.

I stayed in touch with this woman—there were several times I stumbled on a job posting and thought it could be a good fit and sent it on to her, and she always expressed her gratitude to me. Then one day she wrote to me and said, "I thought again about what you said when we first talked, and I'm going back to what I was good at. I'm actually interviewing, and I'm in the final stages."

In the end, I was able to help this person, who I had never met or even heard of, navigate a big detour in her career and find her place. And I did it because she impressed me. I was impressed by how open she was about the process, with me and also with herself. I think that looking back, she might see that period as the time when she grew up, or at least a time when she invested in herself and her learning, as opposed to *Oh my God, I was looking for a job, and I applied to over two hundred companies, and no one got back to me.*

Today, she's on my LinkedIn, and I still follow up with her. Ironically, she just posted something this morning as I'm writing this about a project she's working on and how proud she is to be a part of it. When I read that, I felt proud too. I told myself, *Oh, I was part of her journey. That was cool.*

That's the way you want to leave people feeling. You want them to feel good about their interactions with you. Especially if you're in a small industry. Word gets around, so it helps when the words being spoken about you are positive ones.

People Remember People

An acquaintance of mine recently contacted me to see if I could help her find some high-caliber speakers for an event. I asked her a few questions, and we brainstormed some names, and I asked her, "Who are the people you're targeting? Tell me who you're trying to reach, and I'll see if we have mutual contacts." She gave me a few names, and I recognized one as someone I had interviewed with a very long time ago—like sixteen years ago! I didn't remember how it turned out, whether I didn't take the job or they hired someone else. I just remembered the guy's name, and when I checked LinkedIn, I saw that he and I were connected.

I had no idea how we were connected beyond that one interview. But when I clicked on the message I had sent him, all of a sudden a whole thread opened up. Apparently, I'd closed our meeting in a certain way and wrote to him and told him what I liked and what I didn't. I didn't remember that I had done that, and he probably didn't either! He might not have remembered me at all. But I wrote to him and said, "I have someone who reached out to me because I know you, and I think you would be an amazing speaker for her event. This is who she's working with. Here are the other speakers. Would you be open to helping her? And can I make an introduction?"

He responded, "Yes, absolutely. I'd love to." I don't think he even remembered me, but the fact that the previous correspondence existed was enough for me to feel comfortable reaching out to him. After I read it, I felt good coming back to him, and I think that maybe he responded to me positively because there was some sort of relationship and that I had given him closure.

That's all it takes to make the right kind of impression—taking the time to really see people, thanking them for their time, and treating them well.

Perfecting Your Role Model

Whether or not you've gotten the job, once you've zeroed in on a role, it's time to make the final adjustments that will better position you to fulfill it. We're going to do that now.

1. If you have a job description for this role, you get to skip this step. If you don't, take a few minutes to write your own job description for the role in question or dream job based on everything you know. Make it as complete as you can.

_____

_____

_____

_____

_____

_____

2. Go back to the role model checklist you created in the last chapter, and compare it to the job description.

PRIORITY: 1   2   3   4

JOB DESCRIPTION / REQUIRED CAPABILITIES:

DO I HAVE IT?   YES   NO

IF NOT, HOW DO I CLOSE THE GAP?

PRIORITY: 1   2   3   4

JOB DESCRIPTION / REQUIRED CAPABILITIES:

DO I HAVE IT?   YES   NO

IF NOT, HOW DO I CLOSE THE GAP?

PRIORITY: 1   2   3   4

JOB DESCRIPTION / REQUIRED CAPABILITIES:

DO I HAVE IT?   YES   NO

IF NOT, HOW DO I CLOSE THE GAP?

PRIORITY: 1   2   3   4

JOB DESCRIPTION / REQUIRED CAPABILITIES:

DO I HAVE IT?   YES   NO

IF NOT, HOW DO I CLOSE THE GAP?

3. Prioritize which areas will be most important to your success in the role, and pick the most important one to start. You'll want to focus on the most important things before taking on others.

4. Assess what you need to do to close the gap. Do you need to read something, talk to somebody, learn a skill? Then do whatever that thing is.

5. Refer back to your learning style, and take what you've done one step further—do some further reading, write a LinkedIn post, volunteer your time—so that it really becomes a part of you.

You're almost ready to start from scratch in your new role. In the next and final chapter, we'll deal with something a lot of us tend to forget during tumultuous times—taking care of ourselves, especially our mental health.

CHAPTER 7:

Check Your Baggage

· ·

When you actually execute your plan and your vision, you have everything you need—your partners, the skills, the knowledge, all your metaphorical ducks in a row. But there's one huge component we haven't talked about yet—taking care of yourself. You need to be strong physically but, more importantly, mentally.

Work is an emotional thing. Our careers are such a huge part of our identity and our purpose and take up so much space in our lives, and they can have a powerful effect on our mental health. Starting from scratch usually involves leaving something behind, and sometimes that's not by choice. There might be pain. There might be anger. There might be anxiety about the challenges ahead. And that's all normal, and it's all okay.

What matters is that you find a way to heal and deal with it.

If you're struggling with your mental health, you're not alone. Over 70 percent of the population is suffering from some kind of mental wellness issue—which is actually kind of staggering. Now more than ever, it's crucial to take care of your mental health so that when you start from scratch, you can dedicate 100 percent to the opportunity in front of you without baggage from your past holding you back from everything you can be.

Several years ago I was determined to open my own product management agency. I've been doing this job for so long, working in so many industries, I felt ready to take on the journey of being an independent consultant. I had just left a job in very beneficial circumstances and had a good runway financially to start my own practice from scratch. I started going to events to promote my new business, built my own website, and had two warm introductions to potential first customers. I felt ready.

Then one evening, as I was putting the last finishing touches on my website, I started feeling this weird tingle in my fingers. I shook them and moved on. Several minutes later, the tingle was back, only this time I felt it all over my arm. I started panicking. I was alone at home. What if there was something really wrong? I called a cab and headed to the hospital.

When I arrived at the hospital, I was immediately asked if I could breathe. *Could I?* I couldn't decide, and the room was also spinning. Then I was asked if I have heart issues. None that I knew of. Then I was asked if I'd eaten anything that day. "I didn't," I answered.

All of a sudden, everyone around me looked more relaxed.

"Here, drink this! You had an anxiety attack. Has this ever happened to you before?"

Wow! Anxiety? Me? I thought I had all my ducks in a row.

Looking back, I realize that I'd done everything I needed to do to prep myself for a new journey—everything except listen to my body and take care of myself. I needed to clear my head, regain my strength, and prepare for a new, exciting adventure. And you do, too, even if starting from scratch is the last thing you want to do.

A while ago, I was the head of a big team, and one guy who worked within the organization kept applying to all these different roles on my team. I found this confusing. What exactly was this guy trying to do? Was he trying to jump ship because he didn't like his current job? Did he specifically want to work with me for some reason? That would have been flattering, but the fact that he wasn't focused on a specific role and didn't seem to have a specific passion was very weird to me. Did he not understand the difference between the roles, or the craft of the roles? He had a job—what was his deal?

It wasn't a good indicator.

Since this was an internal candidate, I asked to meet him just to understand what was up. I reached out, and he said, "Great, let's meet." He came to the meeting prepared with a presentation, which I truly appreciated, since I knew he wasn't there to waste my time. He made the extra effort to lay out for me exactly how he would perform the role. Not all the roles he had applied for, just one specific role that I assumed was the role he was most passionate about. I was very curious to see what he had to say.

And, unfortunately, it didn't impress me at all.

Sometimes when a candidate makes a presentation, the presentation lacks the context of the real day-to-day pain the role is supposed to help solve. It's kind of generic. This guy's presentation felt very much like that. It gave me a clear impression that he did not understand what I was looking for and was just presenting his version of what he thought the role needed to be.

Did he not read the job description? Did I not write a clear job description? What was going on?

It was all a little disappointing, because he had a lot of great ideas, and because he had taken the time to create a presentation, I could see his intentions were serious. I suggested he try to do something with those ideas within the organization without switching roles—just to do a little extra work in what amounted to a career "safe space" and get some experience. It's advice I frequently give to younger talent, it worked for me earlier in my career and it seems to work out well for a lot of people. It's a big part of building a role model to prepare to start from scratch, and it was something I thought he would benefit from.

The guy seemed resistant. So I asked him what was stopping him, and he hit me with what felt like a deluge of reasons, all of which were related, all of which came back to some form of disappointment with the organization he had worked for previously. He told the story of how he had worked for this company, and the company was acquired, and his role collapsed, and he wasn't able to do whatever it was that he wanted to do. And then he moved to another role, and he still couldn't really do what he wanted to do. And then this person who could have helped him got fired, and then this person who could have helped moved on. It was just excuse after excuse after excuse. And underneath all of it, I could feel he was carrying this deep, deep disappointment.

It was almost like PTSD.

I realized that through all those changes, he'd never stopped to deal with the pain of losing that first role before he jumped to the next one. He carried that baggage with him. So he ended up doing whatever role he wound up in in a very mediocre way. You could see some passion and life flare up in him from time to time, and then it died, because he wasn't strong enough to give 100 percent of himself to the experience and start that fire.

The conversation affected me. I had seen this same thing at companies where I'd worked before, but I'd never really had the whole experience laid out for me the way he did when he explained his version of why he was where he was. I wanted to help, so I told him I needed some time to think about our meeting and that I would get back to him. And after several days, I did. I said, "I just want to put this in front of you. I want to give it a name. It's something that happens, and you need to handle it, because if you leave now, it will follow you into the next job. It's not that you can't reinvent yourself here anymore. It's that you can't reinvent yourself, period. Something will drag you down the next time. So, either fix it here, or fix it later, but just be aware that you need to fix it."

I could see that his bitterness over what had happened in that role and his baggage over losing it were weighing him down. So I also said, "I actually think that you need a break. You need to reflect on what happened. Understand which part of it was yours, which part of it wasn't, and just let it go."

That was the beginning of my interest in researching this type of PTSD—what is called Posttraumatic layoff disorder, or PTLD—because in my world this happens a lot. I talked a little

> **If you really, truly want to start from scratch, you can't do it while you're still holding on to baggage from your past.**

bit about it in the chapter on resilience, but in this chapter I want to go into more detail about how to deal with the feelings work-related losses tend to generate. Because if you really, truly want to start from scratch, you can't do it while you're still holding on to baggage from your past.

The secret, or at least what seems to have worked for me, is finding some kind of closure before moving on.

How to Find Closure

A few days ago, I was at lunch with some colleagues, including one of my reports who I'd brought with me from WeWork. When he mentioned he had worked there, too, one of my other colleagues said about me, "Oh, she loves WeWork," to which the guy I'd brought over responded, "I actually think she loves *everywhere* she used to work." At first, I thought that was a strange thing to say about me. I definitely didn't love going through all those reorgs, and I haven't been shy about sharing those experiences. But when I look back and reflect on those times, I realize I learned to close those chapters well regardless of what happened to me. Which means that I moved on with an understanding of what I'd learned, both good and bad, and how I grew from the experience. That helped me to start from scratch without any baggage, just some really good memories and validation of my knowledge and experience.. Even the bad memories wound up being good, because once the actual bad experience was over, all that was left was the opportunity for me to change, to grow, to open to something new.

No workplace is perfect, and I've moved through far more jobs than a person in a different field might consider healthy. But I don't feel bad about any of them, because intentionally or not, I was able to find that closure. Whether the thing you're moving on from is a role or a relationship, closure is the thing that keeps you from playing it over and over in your mind, avoiding negative chatter, wondering what you could have done differently or reliving some painful words or other horrible thing that happened to you. It's about going back and understanding what the situation taught you, and then leaving it behind. In the case of a relationship, it's asking, *What did my former partner teach me about love, relationships, and happiness?* If it was a job, it's looking at things like *What were my supervisors, peers, or employees trying to teach me?* In any case, it's asking, *What was the universe trying to teach me?* It's looking back at a situation without blame or emotion and simply asking what you had to learn, where you needed to grow, and whether or not that learning and growth has been accomplished. You wind up with a plan for moving forward more successfully.

That way, when you start from scratch, you leave everything in the past except the things that you've gained. Those you get to keep.

So the next time you have to say goodbye to a role or a person or experience any kind of loss, take yourself out for coffee and have a sincere conversation with yourself. Ask yourself the following:

➔ *What did I accomplish?*

➔ *What did I learn?*

➔ *What was good about it?*

➔ *What would I have changed?*

➔ *What will I do differently next time?*

It's also okay to go back and talk to people and ask for feedback, provided you're willing to be open and listen to what those other people have to say. It won't do you much good if, when someone says, "I would have handled this differently," you get angry or upset. But if you're open to the lesson, it's absolutely okay to go to someone and say, "You know what? I'm not sure what I need to learn from this. Can you help me?" Their answer can give you the guidance you need to move forward, even if it's not what you wanted or expected to hear.

I do this constantly, not just when I'm seeking closure. I remember I once asked for feedback after a meeting, and one comment I got was, "You look much younger than you are in meetings." Which at first offended me. I thought, *Wow, was he talking about my looks or my clothes?* But when I gave myself space to think about the comment instead of simply reacting emotionally and then dismissing it, I realized, *No, he was actually commenting on my behavior.* I realized that I was downplaying my maturity, my experience, and my serious-ness, and that maybe that wasn't having whatever effect I hoped it would have. It wasn't fun to hear. But it gave me something to think about—and to work on if I decide I want to.

Taking care of you starts with that level of reflection, where part of the goal is to pinpoint where you might have gone wrong—not to beat yourself up about it but so you can avoid making the same mistake in the future. It's where you ask yourself, *What was it? Did I not speak to the right people? Did I not show up in this meeting? Was I vigilant enough? Did I give my all in this area?* Because when you're able to pinpoint what went wrong, you give yourself the power to do things differently in the future. When you look at the loss as an opportunity to learn and grow instead of focusing on the rejection, it only makes you stronger.

> When you're able to pinpoint what went wrong, you give yourself the power to do things differently in the future.

Just as you need to learn things before you start a role, give yourself time to learn when you leave one.

. . . .

Change is scary. Even when we use times of change to create a better outcome for ourselves, it's still scary, and many times, even when we do manage to create that better outcome, we step into that new opportunity filled with feelings of self-doubt. This is also called imposter syndrome—and Phyllis Njoroge literally wrote the book about it, titled *From Fraud to Freedom*. As she explains, "When you have a certain background and need to redefine yourself, everything new is scary. It's scary, as you have no idea if you are able and if you are adaptable."

Phyllis and I talked at length about what imposter syndrome feels like, but what I really loved was that while she had a lot of sympathy for IS sufferers, she gave them no discounts. Here is her advice for surviving imposter syndrome when starting from scratch:

> *It's important to acknowledge that feelings aren't facts. "I feel it's out of my league" and "This is out of my league" are not equivalent. But one also needs to acknowledge reality. If you are not good at something, this does not need to be your permanent identity. Yes, play your strengths, but also have a plan to improve your weaknesses.*
>
> *Starting something from scratch will wake up and kick in your imposter syndrome, so it's important to know it's a phase. It passes, but it will come back the next time you move up. There is no such thing as permanently overcoming imposter syndrome.*
>
> *Build self-awareness. Ask yourself and the people you trust for feedback, and work on what you aren't currently good at.*
>
> *Stop and celebrate when you close the gap on something you didn't know or weren't previously good at. And remember that success is a self-reminder when you feel you can't.*
>
> *Don't underestimate self-improvement. Build a plan to work on your weaknesses, don't accept defeat, be particular, and stay consistent about how you execute that plan.*

When I asked Phyllis what she does to work on her mental health, she told me, "When my skip-level manager announced she was leaving, it was a lot to process, so I ended the workday a few hours early. It was important for me to allow myself to not be okay. Some people need to process with others, but I needed to be with myself for a moment. And it's important to not ignore that you're not okay, because those unprocessed feelings just accumulate and express themselves elsewhere. You don't want to blow up just because someone misplaced a spoon," she said with a laugh.

And how did Phyllis spend that "mental health day?"

"I mentally disconnected. I ate a good meal, watched my favorite show on TV, and realized the feeling of chaos was only at work; my life was just fine. Also, therapy and exercise help. One doesn't get up and feel resilient. We all need a support system.

"I read the book *Burnout*, by Amelia and Emily Nagoski. It basically says that to overcome burnout, you need to do three things: 1) do something creative, 2) surround yourself with love, and 3) exercise. I do all those to stay mentally strong. I doodle and journal, meet friends, and exercise. "

But What If You're Not the Person Who Gets Fired?

As I mentioned earlier in this book, work-related PTSD doesn't happen just to the people who lose their jobs. When I was at Verizon and we went through so many rounds of reorganization, some resulting in layoffs, I saw a lot of my peers who stayed behind become dysfunctional. It was fascinating. They were never on the layoff list. They had been really good, talented people who contributed. And suddenly they weren't doing anything anymore. It was like they were suddenly paralyzed; they were unable to execute, unable to concentrate. They just went through the motions, chitchatting and doing busy work all day. Even though they didn't lose their jobs, they lost their ability to do their jobs—or at least do it well.

A lot of those people came to me for advice, because I had been through so many reorgs that I was already emerging as the resident expert in starting from scratch. I kind of felt like a shrink. I remember saying to my husband, "It's like they watched a bomb go off." I didn't know how to help these people. I couldn't figure it out. Was it a kind of survivor syndrome, like people who live through war or a disaster? I started googling and discovered that indeed, postlayoff PTSD includes survivor's guilt for those left behind.

> "Not all storms come to disrupt your life. Some come to clear your path."

I get it. On one hand, it's almost violent to have all these people ripped from your life in a moment. It's upsetting when everything that you know and see every day is suddenly different.

But on the other hand … nothing really happens to you.

The people who survived the layoffs were fine.

In fact, they were better than fine; they just didn't know it. Because when things change, that's when the doors of opportunity open. That's when you can make a choice to start from scratch on your own terms or to rededicate yourself to your current role. You get to decide. Not that every opportunity you take will lead in the direction you expect …

Here's one of my favorite quotes: "Not all storms come to disrupt your life. Some come to clear your path."

When One Door Closes, Another Opens

In one of my early jobs, I made a proposal to my boss. Someone had left a role that was similar to mine, and he was stressed out, so I offered to help him. I said, "You know what? I can do both jobs. And I would hope that when I show you that I can do both, that I actually saved you a full person's salary, you'll be motivated to give me a promotion and a raise."

We shook hands on the deal; he was very happy about my offer, and I got to work. I took on a huge project that the person I was replacing had dropped right in the middle, and when I finished the project, I received several thank-you letters saying I had done a good job. It was tangible proof that my plan had worked, so I forwarded one of those thank-you emails to my boss with a note that said, "I would love to talk to you about this and more." He agreed, and we sat down for a meeting.

While this was very early in my career, I was confident in what I had accomplished. So I reminded him of our agreement and asked him when I should expect to start being compensated as a person who was doing two roles and what that compensation might be. Would I have a salary increase? A better title?

Not exactly. I got ... a lecture!

My boss proceeded to give me a long talk about how I'd done an amazing job but that I'd also proved to him that he was wrong, that it really only should have been one job from the beginning and that he should have given me all that responsibility from the start.

I didn't understand if he was complimenting me or insulting me. What I did understand was that my boss, whom I had just done an enormous favor for and saved an entire person's salary, managed to deliver bad news in a way that also made me feel humiliated and unappreciated. The fact that he said, "I was wrong; you were right" didn't matter. I was very offended. I was sure that I'd done a good job, and he actually kind of said as much. Did he just not appreciate me? Did he not think I was talented enough? Or did he think I was gullible and decide to take advantage of me? Was that it?

I couldn't unpack what was really going on. What was clear was that I knew I did not want to continue working for this person. I did not want to work for someone who was dishonest, or devalued me, or took advantage of me, or all of the above. So I started looking for a job, internally and externally. At first I struggled a little. My confidence had been shaken by the way my boss had treated me, and I didn't really feel inspired. Maybe he had given me a little dose of PTSD—not that, at that point in my career, I had any idea that's what was going on.

I couldn't figure out what could possibly inspire me until I decided I was going to go for it. I was going to apply for a job at one of those big-name companies I fantasized about working for. I never actually thought I'd get the job. In fact, I forgot that I'd even applied. However, three months later, while I was on vacation, they called me. They ended up offering me a job, and that job changed my career path and my life.

And it never would have happened if that boss, pardon my language, had not been an asshole.

When he didn't give me the raise or promotion we agreed to, I didn't get angry or quit. I made the commitment to suck it up until I found a new job, and that meant doing my job and not being bitter about it. I knew the job was there to serve the purpose of paying for my life until I got my next job. But I also had made the decision, based on the way my boss had treated me, that I was not going to stay. I knew it had an endpoint; I just didn't know when that would be. However, that no longer mattered—I had taken control back and saw his behavior as the opportunity I needed to move on.

Looking back, some of the people I met through that job are still my best friends. Some of them are on my PBOD because they're so talented and amazing and I would trust their advice any day. The role itself was amazing and set the stage for me to do other things later in my career. But the rejection—the worst thing that happened to me at that job—was the thing that pushed me past my boundaries. It forced me to think about what I really wanted to do and lit a Spark that made me move a lot faster than I would have if I'd been shown the appreciation I'd expected. If he'd given me that raise, who knows where I'd be today?

Dealing with a boss who isn't honest or respectful also taught me about the importance of workplace culture and norms. From that point on, when I looked at opportunities, I also looked at the culture and the environment. I still do to this day, and when it doesn't work for me, I step away very quickly.

· ·

Mae Singerman is famous for a post that "broke the internet." Somehow she managed to capture something so many people wanted to say, think, allow themselves to do. Over fourteen thousand people reacted to what she wrote.

"I left a job I had for seven years and got a new one. I didn't move up or get promoted. The opposite, actually. I moved out of a management role. I stopped supervising and managing consultants, took a pay cut, no longer had decision-making power over anything significant, and lost my precious director title. In return, I take pride in the daily accomplishments of administrative work. I no longer spend five-plus hours a day in Zoom meetings, work in the evenings, talk to my therapist about work, have email on my cell phone, or stress about taking a day off. With two young kids, a mom with dementia, and an interest in being a human outside of work, it was the right decision."

WOW!

When I asked her what triggered the change, it ultimately came down to her health. "It's been building up, for sure. I'm a helper by nature, and I had a big job. I also carried a lot of the team's emotional energy and took on more official and unofficial responsibilities. With that came low energy at the end of the day, late 10:00 p.m. dinners, and just an overall feeling that there was too much going on. One day I got sick. It was nothing too exotic, but I all of a sudden thought I might have been sick because I'm not happy with my work-life balance and mental health, and with two young kids, a mom with dementia—I had to prioritize that."

Mae was laughing. "You know when you are sick and google your symptoms, and it is always stress related? My illness had zero relation to mental wellness, but I decided it was and that it was a sign I needed change."

Mae was initially looking for a recruiter role, thinking it would be a good starting job that she would be great at because she's excellent with people and loves to connect and help them. But when she researched the field and learned more about the work to be done, Mae realized it wouldn't support the work-life balance she was looking for. So she activated her network and found an administrative role. And it's changed her life.

Part of what enabled Mae to do this was working deliberately and seeking real closure. "I was actually thinking how I'd properly and truly say goodbye. What worked well was a long notice period and a ten-page-long memo for the person who replaced me. Before I left, I was offered to stay on a contract for twenty hours a week, which I knew would never work for me, as I'd again work more.

So we stayed on good terms, and I'm there to support, but as it's not a paid job, we have a healthy relationship of connecting only when it's absolutely necessary. This allows me to really live how I set the plan to be.

"I exercise, eat well; I spend time with my family; I take the day off if my kids are off. Oh, and the biggest change is, I charge my phone in the kitchen and don't wake up with it in my hand!"

Her advice to others? "People don't want to see you miserable, and I was that annoying person complaining all the time, so I took it as a personal mission to make a change. Several years ago, people would think I was crazy for leaving such a big job and making a drastic career change. Now everyone understands or wants to have my courage."

So, does she have any regrets, any second thoughts?

"ZERO! "

. . . .

Dealing with Stress

Stress is basically a given in the business world, especially among high-achieving people who throw all of themselves into their careers. So if it's going to be a factor you can't get rid of, it's crucial to find a way to deal with it.

My friend Jessica Carson, a neuroscience researcher, wrote a book called *Wired This Way* that explores how different types of creators and innovators handle stress. Her research found that each person comes with both light and darkness inside of them. The light is basically the thing that helps them perform—it's where their creativity lies and how they come up with new ideas, new solutions, and new products. But every person has darkness in them, too, and that darkness represents how they deal with bad situations and how stress affects their mental health. Darkness can take different forms. Some people are more prone to anxiety, some develop health issues, some change their behavior. It's all normal and something you can't change. What matters is understanding how you handle stressful situations and how they affect you.

I've discovered that when I'm stressed, I overwork to the point where I exhaust myself and am therefore not able to be my best self. Just having that knowledge is a huge help. When I feel that stress coming, I can say to myself, *Okay, I feel this way, so I know what is going to happen.* And instead of giving in to that urge to work myself to exhaustion, I force myself to do the exact opposite thing and take a day off. That helps me break the pattern.

Whatever you do when you stress out, identifying your own patterns in advance is important to helping you break them, to hold off your darkness and keep it from throwing you off course. That's when you can use different tools—some of which I'll explain in a minute—to help you address your stress and deal with it in a constructive way. Just like your darkness itself, what tools work for you may be different from what works for me. The important thing is to find that thing that works and use it regularly.

Luckily, it's never been easier to find a way to manage your wellness. Right now there are a lot of apps created specifically to help you cope with and overcome stress, with daily programs that teach you and guide you through meditation, help with sleep, track your mood, and more. I'm a big fan of an app called Headspace, which helps me fit meditation into my day, reduce my anxiety, and think more clearly. There are other similar apps out there—Calm and Paradym come to mind—but stress relief doesn't have to come from your phone or any form of technology. Whatever works for you, whether it's talking with a trusted friend or therapist, walking in nature, listening to music, exercise—just as long as it's not self-destructive—it's important to have something in your life that will help you recover from stress.

Another company I love is called Caveday. They facilitated work sessions in a community that keeps you focused and accountable. Another method is called deep work that uses music to calm the brain and get into flow mode so that it doesn't think about too many things at once—something we all have a tendency to do when we're stressed. It helps you narrow your focus so you can concentrate on just one thing and focus on that thing and get it done. I like to use Caveday or deep work music for work that I hate to do, like budget planning. But it's also a great way to turn off all the outside noise and focus on something bigger, like when you need to plan to start from scratch. It's the perfect tool for a brainstorm day, where you can fully focus on your future and not all the little tasks you need to tackle on a daily basis. It can help you cut through all that chatter and noise that take your brain in a million directions and help you focus.

These are Sabela Garcia Cuesta's mental health tips:

"Find inspiration. Find inspiration in the little things in life: a new recipe that you try, a book, an article, or a conversation.

"Express yourself. When you feel frustrated, devastated, upset, or happy and excited—emotions build up. Explore ways to externalize them without hurting other people.

"Set up a goal. Or many little ones. Be aware of what you have accomplished after a determined time frame you set up. The feeling of self-fulfillment is irreplaceable.

"Take risks. If you don't do it, you will regret it forever. If you do it and regret it, at least you experienced it. Worst case scenario: you learn.

"Don't kill your creativity. Don't let yourself get influenced by what people say about your ideas and work. Allow yourself to be playful, test new things, experiment. Even if it doesn't work, at least you had the opportunity to find it out by yourself.

"Work in teams. Find people who like working with you and who stand for the same as you do. Teamwork makes life easier and more enjoyable."

Make a Stress Plan

Stress is going to be a given in your life. What matters is how you deal with it. So take some time to think about the ways you deal with stress and whether or not they are healthy coping mechanisms. If not, look at some of the suggestions in this chapter and try them out.

1. How do you recognize when you are stressed?

_____

_____

_____

2. What helps you unwind?

_____

_____

_____

3. What things have you never tried but are open to trying that can help you deal with stress?

_____

_____

_____

4. Commit here:

Next time I feel _____

I will _____.

SIX STEPS FOR
STARTING FROM SCRATCH

 **ADOPT A LEARNING MINDSET**

 **WORK ON YOUR RESILIENCE**

 BUILD YOUR PERSONAL BOARD OF DIRECTORS

 **spark**

 UNPACK WHO THE NEW YOU WILL BE

 CLOSE KNOWLEDGE GAPS & WORK TOWARDS THE NEW YOU

 GET RID OF BAGGAGE, DON'T DWELL ON THE PAST, LEARN AND MOVE ON

CONCLUSION

It turns out I started writing this book at the perfect time. As I moved into the final chapter, my boss announced that he would be leaving the company. It wasn't a complete surprise—just a few days before, I was talking about him with my husband, and I remember saying, "I wonder how long he'll stay?" So, looking back, the signs (the external spark) were there. And since he was a big asset to the organization, my team, and me, I saw his loss as a net negative for me. On a more granular level, it immediately changed the experience of what my job was. In fact, when I looked back and compared the experience to some of the reorgs I've been through, I realized that the departure of one's immediate supervisor can be pretty close to earthshaking.

It can mean a small reorg with a replacement, but it can also mean a total reimagining of the group's structure that can affect you or your peers' or your reports' future with the company. The effect can be positive, like when there's an opportunity for a promotion, or it can be bad, like a round of layoffs. I've seen many reorgs result in new management bringing in their teams and replacing people for no reason other than wanting the people they trust to come along with them.

And that's all okay. One day maybe you will do it, too, or an ex-manager might ask you to rejoin them at their new gig (hell, I do that all the time!).

What's important in the moment is to recognize that even if it's due to someone else's spark (meaning it's external), you will be starting from scratch. That means it's time to step up your game, learn on your feet, observe opportunities, put yourself forward, and plan the new you.

That's what I'm doing right now, in the wake of this departure. Ironically, a day after I wrote what I thought would be the last word of this book, I decided to leave my job. After a fantastic year at that company, I'm saying goodbye.

Meaning I really, truly am starting from scratch again.

This development has given me a unique opportunity to put my own process to the test. I've been using some of the techniques I've outlined in this book, actively trying to learn all I can about what's going on in my environment, calling on my resilience to deal with the extra stress of this change and its impact on my team, and speaking with several members of my PBOD to get their thoughts and sort through my own. Some of them, knowing how these situations stress me out, offered to meet and help talk through updating my CV and look into other roles where I can gain control back.

I haven't done all these things deliberately—at this point, they are so much a part of how I approach my career that I do most of them automatically. Maybe because change has been a constant in my professional life, I'm always tweaking and adjusting my role model, if not building a completely new one. I'm always working to grow my knowledge in some way, to make myself better at what I do so I'll be ready to start from scratch and able to do it on my terms when the moment comes.

Scary and unwelcome as they can be sometimes, big changes are where the biggest opportunities are hiding. If you can figure out how to harness the moment, you can turn starting from scratch into the engine that powers your career (or your life!) path forward and into new and exciting territory. That's what I've been able to do throughout my career. When everything gets crazy and nobody knows what's coming next, that's when I find a way to thrive—and, more often than not, push myself forward to a new level.

> **Scary and unwelcome as they can be sometimes, big changes are where the biggest opportunities are hiding.**

Since my boss's departure and then mine, meaning after that first external spark happened, I have been in starting-from-scratch mode, following the steps I have outlined in this book. I am in learning mode, I keep in touch with my PBOD, and I'd like to believe that most days I work on maintaining my resilience. Because I wanted to be authentic and in line with what I have written in this book (meaning I need to walk my talk), when I found myself skipping steps, I went back and redid them. Today more than ever, in what feels like the millionth time I am starting from scratch, I feel whole. And I really believe it is because I was accountable to myself. I followed, and continue to follow, the steps outlined in this book.

I unpacked my last experience and the decisions leading to my departure with my boss, peers, and colleagues—and I'm so proud of who I am after this experience. I know what I learned, I know what I accomplished, and I know what I care about and want in my next career more than ever. That led to a conscious decision that I owe it to myself to try once again to work for myself. The last time I did that, I ended up with a severe anxiety attack, but I have grown so much since then. So this time I feel ready, strong, and oriented.

One of the people on my PBOD, Inbar, is a creative director I have been working with for the past ten years. Despite the fact that she is based in Israel and I am in New York, we manage to keep in touch and talk often. When I updated her about what was happening and told her what I wanted my next role to be, she actually screamed, "Are you for real? Me too!" After several conversations, we decided to join forces. We started a product strategy and design agency together and named it Dragons Can Fly. Being the creative genius she is, Inbar also created a profile pic for me, one in which I'm wearing the headpiece of a dragon warrior. It made me laugh while also making me feel empowered and again a part of something I cared about.

We each wrote our personal role models, and to close the gap on our role models' capabilities, we started reading, watching videos, taking courses, listening to podcasts, and sending each other content and things to learn from. We also met exciting people together and apart and came back to report about new learnings and ideas.

Then, together, we wrote our company's role model while also managing to land several customers. I learned that companies also have role models, and as partners, Inbar and I need to work on our resilience. When one of our customers reached a big milestone, we talked about the stress of launching our own business and decided to set boundaries and find ways to support each other.

During my part of the presentation to the client, I received a text message. I saw it was from Inbar and decided I needed to look at it in case she wanted me to say something I forgot.

The text read as follows: "You are doing an amazing job!"

At that moment, I realized I'd chosen the right partner for this leg of the ride. She was aware of my mental health and what I needed right then and there. After we won another big account, she texted me: "I'm going to celebrate! What are you doing this evening?" She's good at maintaining her own resilience—and mine too! Is this what I'm going to do when I grow up? I know I'm in a good place now; if a spark shows up, I might again start from scratch, and that's totally OK.

I hope, by documenting the steps I take when I start from scratch, I've helped give you a new perspective and a new sense of your own power when these things happen to you. Because they will. Organizational changes are unavoidable, but they're also survivable. And they're not only survivable—they're full of the kinds of hidden possibilities that make great careers happen.

They've certainly been key to mine.

Right now, I am collecting stories of other people who have started from scratch, and I'd love to hear yours. You can share it with me and other people who are interested in this topic, or just read other people's stories for inspiration, at www.startingfromscratchthebook. com.

ACKNOWLEDGMENTS

I never really told him, but my dad probably had the biggest influence on my career. He passed away over ten years ago, and he was a pro at starting from scratch. He had his own company and worked as a civil engineer, and I remember my parents' conversations about the market's ups and downs and how they affected him. He always got back on his feet and would start from scratch, winning another big contract. He passed away at the age of eighty, working to his last day. My mom started her second career at the age of fifty (I was fifteen). I remember her studying late at night, preparing for tests, and attending conferences, and I remember how happy she was as her new clinic started to grow. She is now eighty-two, and she still works. I guess starting from scratch is in my DNA—thanks Dad and Mom!

My husband, Eliad, started his life and career from scratch because I wanted us to move to the United States. At the age of thirty-six, he overhauled everything he knew about his life, surroundings, friends, and later also his career. He is the first to entertain a conversation when I have a spark to start from scratch. He is also the person who pushed me to write this book—a gift I'll cherish forever. Thank you, my love.

My daughters, Healey and Libby, my resilience and strength. You already started from scratch when at the ages of five and almost three you moved to a new country, not knowing the language, and you aced it. When one day you need to start from scratch, remember that you already did it so well. It's in your DNA, and I will always be here, rooting for you. I love you monkeys!

I want to thank the many people who opened their hearts and shared with me their starting-from-scratch stories. Many of them are mentioned in this book and on my website: Hilla Bakshi, Carrie Collins, Melissa Cohen, Sabela Garcia Cuesta, Jonaed Iqbal, Eugina Jordan, Mariana Kobayashi, Lisa Mayer, Phyllis Njoroge, Ashwini Panse, Kathryn Parsons, Liliana Petrova, May Piamenta, Maria Rosati, Landon Sanford, Mae Singerman, Prabhdeep Singh, Sarena Straus, Mrinalini (Mili) Iyengar, Jillian Tirath, Kay Koehler, and Janet Brewer. I also want to thank the whole women's network at Chief: ladies, thank you for always having my back, a brain to pick, a listening ear, and a shoulder to lean on. Thanks, Carolyn Childers and Lindsay Kaplan, for building the table.

I want to thank the many people I interviewed in order to know how to write a book: Lori Bongiorno, Tal Ben-Shahar, Dror Poleg, Lisa Gable, Rob Napoli, Elizabeth Rosenberg, Michelle Ferguson, and Bobbi Wegner—thanks for helping me learn. Lisa and Bobby—thank you for mastering starting from scratch so well and being a part of my book.

Thank you, Gil Peretz, for being my mentor from the age of fourteen, teaching me that the support and advice of knowledgeable people is something I should always seek. Thanks for the beautiful foreword. It's such a beautiful closure to thirty-plus years of friendship.

Thank you to Lisa Canfield, Bonnie Hearn Hill, and the Advantage Media team—Olivia Tanksley, Megan Elger, Josh Houston, Analisa Smith, and Alison Morse—for your support and love for *Starting from Scratch* even before I wrote the first word.

Thanks to Inbar Edut for your partnership, friendship, and your wonderful tips that make my book cover so great.

To my (almost biological) sisters, Judi Badnani and Netalie Linden, for playing the role of the blindly loving personal board of directors so well.

To my bosses, mentors, and peers: I'm different because I met you. Whether it was fate or lucky coincidence, I'm glad we've met. Special love to Dermot McCormack and Nicole Oge. To Bill Pence and Steve Hans, my legendary managers and mentors, for seeing the force of nature in me and trusting my way, may you rest in peace.

Thanks to everyone who supported my book launch, commented on my posts, and sent emails and messages. I am inspired by you.

ABOUT THE AUTHOR

Osnat is a product leader, strategist, and builder and an active advisor and coach for startups and young professionals. Over her twenty-plus-year career in product management, she cofounded Dragons Can Fly, a product strategy and design agency, and led product partnerships for BBG Ventures and product and innovation groups for AOL Studios and Verizon. As part of the founding team at WeWork Labs, she helped build the company's physical and digital experiences, and she most recently served as senior vice president of Product Management at Diligent. In 2021, Osnat was selected as one of the product-led-growth top 25 influencers and currently serves on the advisory board for Audioburst and for Computer Science at Hunter College, and is an alumni committee member at the American Friends of Tel Aviv University. She's an advocate for resilience and mental health in the workplace and a founding member of Chief, a network focused on connecting and supporting women executive leaders. Osnat lives with her family in NYC. *Starting from Scratch* is her first book. For more starting-from-scratch go to www.startingfromscratchthebook.com

CPSIA information can be obtained
at www.ICGtesting.com
Printed in the USA
JSHW041255131222
34824JS00001B/92